THE ENGLISH MUMMERS

AND THEIR PLAYS

UNIVERSITY OF PENNSYLVANIA
PUBLICATIONS IN FOLKLORE AND FOLKLIFE

Editor: Kenneth S. Goldstein; *Associate Editors:* Dan Ben-Amos,
Tristram Potter Coffin, Dell Hymes, John Szwed, Don Yoder;
Consulting Editors: Samuel G. Armistead, Maria Brooks, Daniel
Hoffman, David Sapir, Biljana Šljivić-Šimšić

HENRY GLASSIE
*Pattern in the Material Folk Culture
of the Eastern United States*

ALAN BRODY
*The English Mummers and Their Plays:
Traces of Ancient Mystery*

PIERRE MARANDA AND ELLI KÖNGÄS MARANDA, EDITORS
Structural Analysis of Oral Tradition

THE ENGLISH MUMMERS AND THEIR PLAYS

TRACES OF ANCIENT MYSTERY

ALAN BRODY

UNIVERSITY OF PENNSYLVANIA PRESS
Philadelphia

PR
635
.F6
B7
1970

1664

TO ALEX HELM

With gratitude and admiration

Who lists may in their Mumming see
Traces of ancient mystery.

Sir Walter Scott, MARMION

I say that the stage is a concrete physical place which asks to be filled, and to be given its own concrete language to speak.
I say that this concrete language, intended for the sense and independent of speech, has first to satisfy the senses, that there is a poetry of the senses as there is a poetry of language, and that this concrete physical language to which I refer is truly theatrical only to the degree that the thoughts it expresses are beyond the reach of the spoken language. Antonin Artaud [1]

In his great and prophetic book, *The Theater and Its Double,* Antonin Artaud speaks of the need to cut through the tyranny of language and rediscover the true relationship between ritual and drama. Action has been supplanted by explanation in our Western civilization, he suggests; we have tried to remove ourselves from the limitless and terrifying possibilities of existence by surrounding them with artificial forms. As another critic has put it, we have tried to reduce the mystery of consciousness to a soluble problem. [2]

There is in England, however, a seasonal performance in which we can still discern traces of that ancient mystery. The men's dramatic ceremonial, commonly known as the mummers' play, has roots which extend deep into a ritual past. On one night of the year the men of certain towns disguise themselves and form a troupe which visits certain pre-arranged stations. At each one the men perform a little play which, in spite of its historical permutations and variant versions from village to village, consists of a certain common cluster of actions. No matter how fragmented, modernized, expanded, or overlaid with literary accretions there is invariably a figure who dies and is resurrected.

It is from this basic action of death and resurrection that our investigation of the mummers' play will begin.

This is a particularly opportune time in the history of the theater to examine a phenomenon like the mummers' play. In the major theater centers of America and Europe today a marked emphasis on the ritualistic qualities of the dramatic event has developed. The question of the relationship between actor and audience, the nature of the playing area, the very purpose of the performance itself, in terms of immediate or imaginative change—all these questions so central to an understanding and appreciation of the mummers' play, are precisely the questions we are challenged with by companies such as The Living Theater, Jerzy Grotowski's Theater Laboratory of Poland, Eugenio Barba's *Odin Teatret* in Norway, and the Bread and Puppet Theater in New York. When the Bread and Puppet Theater performs within the improvised circle of the stage in the streets of New York it gives us a new awareness of ourselves as a community, one with a vested moral and political interest in the action. When The Living Theater mounts *Paradise Now,* it means it. The company attempts to effect an immediate experience of reunification unhampered by literary distance. There is a direct, ritualistic purpose informing the evening. Peter Brook stages Seneca's *Oedipus* in a conventional proscenium theater, but he trains his actors to find the incantatory quality of the language first.

It is the ritualistic elements of dramatic events like these which have caused much of the consternation in audiences weaned on a theater of realism and language. For these reasons I hope my study will prove helpful and suggestive, not only to the student of folklore, but of drama as well.

It is in my final chapter that I attempt to deal most explicitly with the possible relationship between myth, ritual, and the mummers' play. I suspect that my suggestions here may come under the most severe critical attack. I welcome that. Until fairly recently the men's ceremonial has received little scholarly attention. If my thoughts can generate debate and further investigation I shall consider them fruitful.

My thesis is based, simply, on the idea that drama, as explained action requiring some separation between performer and audience, can emerge from ritual at any stage of religious consciousness. There are three distinct types of men's ceremonial: the Hero-Combat, the Sword Play, and the Wooing Ceremony. These three types represent the development of drama out of a single ritual at three different stages of development. I do not mean to suggest that these stages are a part of any kind of evolutionary development in sophistication, as though there were some kind of moral or intellectual hierarchy of religious consciousness, or, just as naively, that there is some universal timetable of cultural growth. Men have, however, used markedly different forms of expression to celebrate their consciousness, and those differences do have correspondences in the separate structures of the three types of men's ceremonial.

To expand on this theory I have drawn, in large part, on the Cambridge scholars and their studies of Greek ritual and drama. I am aware that many folklorists find the Cambridge school outdated, but I have chosen to build on their work rather than that, say, of the modern structural anthropologists, because of the careful attention figures such as Harrison, Cornford, Murray, and Binney have given to dramatic theory. The Cambridge school has limitations; it is also rich with suggestive insight. I have tried to take those limitations into account without losing the very real values of the approach. If nothing else, as I say in Chapter VI, Jane Ellen Harrison offers a viable vocabulary. F. M. Cornford, on the other hand, offers a brilliant, extended analysis of the ritual aspects of a dramatic structure astonishingly similar to the mummers' play in *The Origin of Attic Comedy.*

The method, then, with all its dangers, is analogy. I am not trying to establish any kind of direct, causal relationship between Greek ritual and the mummers' play. I have made no attempt to trace the play back to any concrete, historical source.

Those who find my final discussion too "literary" will, I hope, find something of value in the rest of the book, where I have tried to give a fairly straightforward account of the nature of the three types of men's ceremonial.

Much of the material here is based on my study of the late Alex Helm's superb collection in Congleton, Cheshire. I first met Mr. Helm in the summer of 1966. Since that time my indebtedness for his generosity, my admiration for his careful, committed scholarship, and my affection for him, as well as for Mrs. Helm, his daughter, Alison, and his son, Ian, have continued to grow. In our discussions of the play while I was in England, through the mail when I returned to America, and during the time that this manuscript was in preparation he proved a challenging critic and uncompromising taskmaster. I was fortunate to have such a person as a friend and it is for these reasons that I have dedicated this book to him.

I am grateful, also, to Dr. Samuel F. Johnson, who first sponsored this study as a doctoral dissertation at Columbia University and saw it through two years of research, writing, and revision with me; to Dr. Theodor Gaster, not only for his brilliant work in folklore and anthropology upon which I have drawn so heavily, but for his personal support and encouragement; to Dr. Howard Schless and Dr. Daniel Dodson of Columbia University for their careful reading and valuable criticism; to the National Endowment for the Humanities and Skidmore College for their financial assistance; to Dr. Alan Gailey, keeper of the Ulster Folk Museum, for his generosity and the insights he afforded into the Irish versions of the play; to Miss E. M. Loughram of the Folk-Lore Society Library at the University of London; to Mrs. June Molava, whose care and accuracy with the manuscript has saved me months of work; to Mr. Norman Peacock for permission to reprint his text of the Greatham Sword Play; to Dr. Maud Karpeles for permission to quote from Cecil Sharp's Field Notebooks; to The Folklore Society for permission to quote from The Ordish Collection, and to the many other dedicated collectors whose work has made this preparation of this book such an exciting and illuminating experience.

I must also thank my wife, Paula, for her patience, her coffee, and her stamina in reading every draft this work has seen. Finally, I am grateful to my children, Lise and Dylan, for respecting the deep, ritual significance of the closed study door.

August 1969   A. B.

CONTENTS

ILLUSTRATIONS

THE ENGLISH MUMMERS
AND THEIR PLAYS

ABBREVIATIONS

BSA	Annual of the British School at Athens
CNQ	Cheshire Notes and Queries
CR	Classical Review
DJ	The Durham University Journal
DNQ	Devon and Cornwall Notes and Queries
FL	Folk-Lore
FLJ	Folk-Lore Journal
JAF	Journal of American Folklore
JDA	Journal of the Derbyshire Archaeological and Natural History Society
JEFDS	Journal of the English Folk Dance Society
JEFDSS	Journal of the English Folk Dance and Song Society
JHS	Journal of the Hellenic Society
KCJ	Kent County Journal
MP	Modern Philology
NQ	Notes and Queries
ODF	Oxfordshire and District Folklore Society Annual Record
PMLA	Publication of the Modern Language Association
RMC	Rutland Magazine and County Historical Record
SAC	Sussex Archaeological Collection
SP	Studies in Philology
TDR	Tulane Drama Review
TLCA	Transactions of the Lancashire and Cheshire Antiquarian Society
TSA	Transactions of the Shropshire Archaeological and Natural History Society
TWAS	Transactions of the Wisconsin Academy of Science
TYDS	Transactions of the Yorkshire Dialect Society
WA	Wiltshire Archaeological and Natural History Magazine
WRUB	Western Reserve University Bulletin

ONE

INVESTIGATING THE ACTION

Trying to deal with a study of the mummers' play is like trying to sort out hundreds of different sets of fingerprints. Except for some basic differences which can help separate them into three fairly distinct classes, every one has the same, easily recognizable shape. Yet no two are exactly alike. This is one of the most maddening and, at the same time, fascinating aspects of the play. In one way it is also the most helpful. For, as one reads further and further into the enormous number of plays that have been collected since the seventeenth century from villages throughout England, Ireland, and Scotland, he discovers that no matter how many variations are rung on the same theme, the basic action remains constant. Still further, as the variations multiply, so the mummers' play comes to define itself and its own unique identity more and more clearly. Every new version we come upon simply forces us back to the core of the play.

There are only two elements that we can safely say all the hundreds of texts and fragments collected so far have in common.[A] They are all seasonal and they all contain a death and resurrection somewhere in the course of their action.

[A] The definitive collection of play texts is the thirty-five-volume Helm Collection which will be discussed later in the chapter. Thirty-one of these volumes consist of play texts and collected scholarship and criticism. The remaining four are indexes.

When referring to texts I shall give the original bibliographical data as well as its location in the Helm Collection. The latter will be indicated by an H.C. preceding volume and page number. If the citation is from the index, it will be according to village, county and page.

If no original source is cited, the text is found only in Helm.

3

One other difficulty here, however, is the use of the term "mummers' play" itself. "Mummers" is both imprecise and misleading. In the West Riding of Yorkshire and East Lancashire, children with blacked faces go from house to house at Christmas time, sweeping the hearth and accompanying their work with little humming noises. They are called mummers, but they have nothing to do with any kind of performance, unless we consider the odd little ritual task they perform a primitive version of the Happening. At the same time, there are records of troupes of performers all over England who came out, or are still coming out, every year to perform precisely the action we are discussing and who have never heard of the term "mummers." They call themselves "guizers," "plough jacks," "Jolly Boys," "Paper Boys," and a host of other names which E. K. Chambers has sorted out and reproduced in a dizzying list.[1]

It is not quibbling to say that the title "mummers' play" is inadequate and misleading for a fresh study of this particular form of folk drama. The term is misleading not only because it is so easy to confuse it with the courtly mummings of the fourteenth and fifteenth centuries,[2] but because of the connotation of silence the word "mummer" carries.

Much, too, has been made of the word's derivation from the Dutch *momme* and Danish *mumme,* meaning "to disguise oneself with a mask." [3] Disguise may well emerge as a key element, but again, it would be unfair to assume too much from a name that is used for only a limited number of plays otherwise so widespread throughout England.

I propose, therefore, to use the overall term, "men's dramatic ceremony," as it is used by Alex Helm, Norman Peacock, and E. C. Cawte in *English Ritual Drama.*[4] I propose to use as well their division of the ceremony into the three fairly distinct categories: the Hero-Combat, the Sword Dance Ceremony, and the Wooing Ceremony. These are valuable distinctions and somewhat more precise than Chambers' classification of Hero, Sword, and Plough Play,[5] which tends to place the emphasis on a plough that is not always present and to disregard the importance of the wooing action which is a constant element in ceremonies that do not follow the shape of the other two.[B]

[B] T F. Ordish, "Folk Drama," *FL,* II (1891), 314–335, divides the play into Mummers', Plough, and Pace Egg. This is even less helpful since it gives so much weight to the Pace Egg, which is clearly nothing more than a seasonal variant of the Hero-Combat action, as is the Cheshire Souling Play, which he does not deal with at all.

This study, then, will deal with the men's dramatic ceremony in England, a seasonal performance in which is enacted the death and resurrection of one or more of the characters.

The Three Types

Although we will be going more deeply into the structure of the three different types of ceremony in later chapters, let us look briefly at the major characteristics here so that we are clear from the beginning about just what kinds of action we are speaking.

The Hero-Combat is the most familiar type of ceremony, in which a protagonist meets an antagonist in direct combat. One of the two falls and is subsequently revived by a third party who acts as a doctor. There are never less than three performers in the Hero-Combat, although there can be many more, as well as a multiplicity of combats, deaths, and resurrections.[c] Most of the time there are other elements involved in the action such as a prologue, challenges, and counter-challenges, a lament, a cure boast by the doctor and a *quête,* about which we shall have a great deal to say later. It is, however, only the combat, the death, and the revival which give this particular type of ceremony its shape.

There are two obvious points separating the Hero-Combat from the Sword Dance Ceremony. The first is the linked sword dance itself, never performed by fewer than five men. The second is the manner of death, which does not arise from a direct, hand-to-hand combat, but from the action of the community of dancers on a single character. In most cases this is effected by placing a "lock" of swords around the neck of the victim and each of the dancers suddenly and simultaneously withdrawing his own weapon.

The third type of ceremony, peculiarly confined to the East Midland counties of Rutland, Lincolnshire, Leicestershire, and Nottinghamshire, is the Wooing Ceremony. This play, too, has its combat between two opponents, a death and resurrection. Here, however, it does not appear to be the central, significant action. Although it occurs in one form or

---

Joseph Needham and Arthur L. Peck, "Molly Dancing," *JEFDSS,* I (December 1933), 80, raise other objections to Ordish's classification.

[c] In Ross on Wye, Herefordshire, for instance, St. George slays no less than seven antagonists and is finally slain himself by the doctor. Ella Mary Leather, *Folk Lore of Herefordshire* (Hereford, 1912), pp. 141–146. H.C., II, 183–186.

another in every example, the combat can happen anywhere and at any-time during the performance, and it can be between any two players.[D] It is, rather, the wooing action itself which emerges as the significant, constant element from the eighty-five examples we have of this type. There is always a "female" here, who, however fragmented the action, is wooed and won by a clown.[E] A second, older "female," often carrying a bastard child whose fatherhood she tries to assign to the clown, is also common. She is, unfortunately, not a constant factor, although she may have been before fragmentation and the outright bowdlerization of which we have some evidence.[F] Nevertheless, it is the introduction of the sexual theme in the wooing of the lady that is the distinctive feature of this type of ceremony.

Two other features worth noting here are the fact that all the Wooing Ceremonies are confined to the East Midland counties and the New Year season. The Hero-Combat, on the other hand, exists everywhere, including the East Midlands, and is found as the Pace Egg Play at Easter and the Soul-Cakers Play at All Souls.

The Scholarship

The history of scholarship concerned with these men's dramatic cere-monies is a fascinating one and clearly explains the need for taking a fresh look at them.

Throughout the eighteenth and nineteenth centuries, the few col-

[D] In Somerby, Lincolnshire, the Recruiting Sergeant and the Indian King fight. Margaret Macnamara, "A Christmas Mummers' Play," *Drama,* X (December 1931), 42–44. H.C., XVI, 320–323.

In Carlton-le-Moorland, Beelzebub kills Dame Jane. "Memories," LCL (February 3, 1934), 14. H.C., III, 413–420.

Elsewhere, combatants include Tom Fool, Old Threshing Blade, The Lady (a character distinct from Dame Jane), Bold Tom, Eesum Squeesum, and Bold Black.

[E] The term "female" is used to denote the female character portrayed by the male player. The usual term is "man-woman" but this connotes an hermaph-roditic nature which is a distortion. The player who takes the part of the Lady or Dame Jane is representing a woman, not a half-man.

[F] See pp. 83–86 on the difference between Sharp's version of the Ample-forth Play in *Sword Dances,* III (London, 1912), 50–76, and the original ver-sion in the Field Notebooks. See also Chapter Five below for the influence of the Elizabehan Jig on the Wooing Ceremony.

lected texts that did exist lay unnoticed in the pages of obscure local histories and antiquarian collections of folk customs. In these, attention was never focused on the play itself. Their performance was generally brought in as another example of the quaint or even sinful ways of the folk. The Reverend Henry Bourne, for instance, originally wrote his *Antiquitates Vulgares* in 1725 as a diatribe against, of all things, the popish practices of the people. This particular work is now considered the first major document of the nineteenth century folklore revival.[6] This book was later edited and expanded by John Brand into the antiquarian classic, *Observations on Popular Antiquities.* In neither of these collections does a complete play appear, although it is in Brand that we find the first allusion to the *Revesby Play,* perhaps the best-known and most mysterious play yet collected (see Appendix D). There are other works of the same type, however, in which we do find actual texts reproduced. George Ormerod, the Cheshire historian, reproduced fragments of a Hero-Combat in *The History of the County Palatine of Chester* in 1818.[7] Hone, in *The Every Day Book* of 1826, gave us another version of the Hero-Combat[8] and Robert Chambers still another in the *Book of Days,* 1869.[9] All three, upon investigation, prove to be taken from chapbook versions of the play.

Margaret Dean-Smith describes these scattered nineteenth century textual sources with characteristic humor and tolerance as local histories which commonly have an introductory chapter on manners and customs; then annotations to collections of "rare manuscripts and scarce poems," published by antiqarian societies; and finally, "the itineraries of those who set out to see the Indian revival, or failing the Grand Tour went in search of the Picturesque in the wilder parts of Britain." [10]

Chapbooks, too, were still in vogue in the nineteenth century. In places as widely separated as London, Manchester, Leeds, and Belfast, publishers ground out pamphlets such as *The Peace Egg or St. George's Annual Play for the Amusement of Youth; St. George and the Turkish Knight, A Christmas Joust for Boys,* and *Walker's New Mummer or, The Wassail Cup. A Romance Showing how the four brave patron saints conquered the renowned Pagan Giant Saladin. Written expressly for all mummers, to commemorate the holy wars and the happy festival of Christmas.* Until the 1850's, then, the only printed sources for the texts of the performances were the isolated local histories, antiquarian collections and commercial chapbooks.

In the latter half of the century, however, folklore, and the men's ceremonial as part of it, began to emerge as a significant field of scholarly inquiry. It was during this time that Thoms began his pioneering work with the publication of the first issue of *Notes and Queries,* reproducing innumerable play texts between 1850 and 1880, while he was still editor. During the same period the newly organized Folk Lore Society published the series, *County Folk Lore from Printed Sources.* This was an attempt to pull together all the diverse, unfocused material in the histories and collections of the earlier part of the century as well as the more recent local dialect dictionaries and glossaries which invariably held hidden veins of folk culture, and often ceremonial texts.

Still, however, no specific attention was paid to the play by itself. When the Cambridge scholars took their lead from the work of Frazer and Mannhardt and began looking at the roots of Greek culture in primitive belief and custom, there was an occasional, parenthetical mention of the men's ceremonial in Great Britain as similar to the hypothetical ritual which they believed shaped the myths of figures like Dionysus and Osiris, but this was invariably nothing more than a preoccupied nod. The only exception in the Cambridge school was E. H. Binney, whose incisive and extraordinarily advanced thinking on the folk drama we shall have occasion to look at in more detail.

The first published attempt to isolate the play and collect all the extant examples for serious, focused study was made by R. J. E. Tiddy. It was a tragically abortive one. Tiddy was killed in World War I. His book, *The Mummers' Play,* was published posthumously in 1923, a brilliant study but fragmentary, including only thirty-one versions of the play.

By this time, work in the entire field of folklore had accelerated to such a degree that only ten years later Chambers was able to publish a bibliography of 159 texts in *The English Folk Play.*[11] Chambers had earlier devoted a chapter of *The Medieval Stage* to the folk drama but his later work marked the first full-length study to be published on the men's ceremonial.

In writing *The English Folk Play,* Chambers was able to draw on the work of Cecil Sharp, who had been collecting and publishing examples of the English sword and morris dance since 1906. Sharp was not so much interested in the drama as in the choreography of the dance itself. His three volumes on *The Sword Dance of Northern England* did, however, contain some key texts.

Even before Sharp was collecting dances in the Cotswolds and northern England, T. F. Ordish was concentrating exclusively on collecting all the extant versions of the play. Although the Ordish collection was completed by the time Chambers began work on *The English Folk Play,* Chambers was apparently unaware of its existence. The Ordish collection consists of over six hundred versions of the play, including many wooing texts which would probably have influenced Chambers' attitude toward it. It would have been difficult for Chambers to dismiss the Wooing Ceremony as he does, calling it a simple variant of the Sword Dance Play (an awkward position to maintain even in the light of only the nine versions Chambers had at his disposal), and describing the wooing element itself as a late accretion of some independent literary play.

The Ordish collection did not finally become available for study until about ten years ago with the work of Alex Helm. Helm, whose major interest at the time was the Morris dance, had just begun to collect versions of the Cheshire Soul-Cakers Play at the suggestion of Margaret Dean-Smith, the librarian for the English Folk Dance and Song Society. Through a collector named K. J. Holland, Helm traced the Ordish papers to Alan Gomme. Gomme was delighted to have somebody sort and arrange the material in his possession. The papers arrived at Helm's Cheshire home in a thoroughly chaotic state; manuscripts, clippings, handwritten scraps, some illegible, some illiterate, all jumbled together in large crates. Helm proceeded to organize the material according to county and town and finally presented the Folk Lore Society with four superb volumes of work. Having completed the organization of Ordish's work, Helm, along with Norman Peacock, R. J. Marriott, and E. C. Cawte, continued the work of collecting and organizing all the extant versions of the play into a collection, in which the Ordish papers comprise volumes V–VIII. This collection is now housed in Helm's private library in Congleton, Cheshire.[12]

With the historical documentation, the collected criticism, and the new texts brought together in the Helm collection, it is now possible to take a fresh look at the men's dramatic ceremonial. The collection closes many gaps in our knowledge of the history of the play, its development and its form. It also makes it possible to clarify and define for ourselves the questions that still remain unanswered, even though it may not give us the answers themselves. This may even be its greatest contribution, for it points the direction to further, even more fruitful critical examination.

The Play as an Action

The first problem that becomes clear is the difficulty of any kind of literary approach to the play. Arthur Beatty,[13] T. F. Ordish,[14] and E. H. Binney,[15] as well as Helm, himself,[16] have all made a point of viewing the play only as an action. Margaret Dean-Smith stated this position most clearly and directly. "The Play," she said, "and any significance it may have, resides in the action: the text is a local accretion, often both superfluous and irrelevant—the Play can exist in action alone without a word spoken." [17] Certainly no one would quarrel with the idea that if it were primarily the language, or even the specific story the language tells, that was the focus of serious investigation, the men's ceremonial could be dismissed as trivial. Douglas Kennedy has pointed out that there is a certain "folksy" charm about the simplicity and rustic humor of the texts,[18] but that alone would hardly render the play worthy of the kind of extensive, serious consideration it has received. It is, rather, in *what the performers are doing* that the richness of the play lies.

The difficulty here is that it is mainly in this superfluous text that the bulk of our evidence about the nature of the men's ceremonial lies. Few of us have been fortunate enough to see the seasonal ceremony performed in its proper setting. It is even probable that the majority of those who have were not seeing a traditional troupe.[G] We are thrown into the dilemma of having to rely heavily on textual evidence for a non-literary event, the frozen, brittle page for information about a fluid, constantly changing transition. This is the trap that Chambers fell into in *The English Folk Play* when he spent so much time tracing lines and whole scenes to literary sources.[19] No matter how many words and scenes the ceremony accrues, loses, or juxtaposes, it is all no more than the water breaking, shifting, and receding around the rocklike center of the action. It is this center of action that we must deal with if our study is to have any value.

The Problem of History

The second basic problem in a study of the development of the play lies in the lack of historical documentation.

[G] According to Alex Helm there are only about five or six traditional Hero-Combat troupes left today.

Even by admitting the questionable evidence of a manuscript dated 1800, which purports to be reproducing an earlier work, we can only push our first substantial account back to 1685. This account reads,

> on our new green last evening here was presented the drollest piece of mummery I ever saw in or out of Ireland. There was St. George and St. Dennis and St. Patrick in their buffle coats and the Turks likewise and Oliver Cromwell, and a doctor and an old woman who made rare sport till Beelzebub came in with a frying pan upon his shoulder and a great flail in his hand threshing about him on friends and foes, and at last running away with the bold usurper whom he tweaked by his gilded nose—and then came a little Devil with a broom to gather up the money that was thrown to the Mummers for their sport. It is an ancient pastime they tell me of the citizens.[20]

It might be noted, too, that there is no mention of the key death and resurrection here, although the presence of familiar figures like St. George, the Turk, Oliver Cromwell, Beelzebub, and the little Devil with a broom, lead us to regard this passage as an account of the Hero-Combat type of ceremony.

This is a bizarre situation and certainly one of the most mysterious aspects of the play. Before the Cambridge scholars suggested the idea that the play might be the fragmented remains of a pre-Christian ceremony, the general belief was that it had its genesis in some medieval mystery or morality play which had been transformed over the years into a mindless, seasonal charade by the folk. But even if its earliest appearance had occurred as late as the fourteenth and fifteenth centuries, why has there not been any evidence found which we can point to with any certainty as a reference to the men's ceremonial? Why do we have to wait until the end of the seventeenth century, when it had already, apparently, degenerated into simply "the drollest piece of mummery"?

There are earlier references through the fifteenth and sixteenth centuries to "mummers," "morris dancers" or "players," and even to Robin Hood Plays,[21] but not one of them affords evidence about our men's ceremonial, and certainly nowhere do we find a hint of the all-important death and resurrection. Tantalizing extracts like the following appear in abundance, but they cannot be said to apply with certainty to the men's ceremonial.

Gyftis and Rewardes

December 1560	To George, Mr. Pellam's man, to furnish himmselfe lord of Chrismas and his men in a lyvery. 40s
January 1560–1	To Frauncis Cowper . . . besides 50s by my ladies Grace and Pretie, for the furniture of the lord of Christmas 6s 2d
	To George, he lorde of good order, for my Master's gift to him 10s
	To one of Borne which brought a bayting bull 3s 4d
February	"To one which played the hobby-horse before my master and my ladies Grace." 6s 8d
March	"To the waytes of Lincolne, the 12th daie" 20d
August	"To two men which played upon the puppets two nights before her Grace." 6s 8d
September	To four musicians and a hobby-horse which weare at Beleawe at the marriage of Mr. Carr and Deniman 15s 10d
December	To two of my Lorde Robert dudleis men which came to playe before them uppon the drume and phiph 6s
1561–2	
May	"To a morrisse dawncer of little Bytam 2s
July	"To the waightes of Lyncolne inrewarde for playinge 3s 4d [22] [H]

"Morrisse dawnce" or some variant of it, is a term used again and again during the fifteenth and sixteenth centuries, but always in maddeningly vague reference to some kind of performance by some kind of players or dancers on some kind of occasion. The same is true of phrases like "to one which played the hobby-horse." Nowhere before the alleged Dublin

[H] Frederick George Lee, "Oxfordshire Christmas," *NQ*, 5th s., II (December 26, 1874), 503–505, records an Oxfordshire Play he witnessed "by those whose custom it had been, from time immemorial, to perform it at the house of the gentle-people of that neighborhood at Christmas, between St. Thomas's Day and Old Christmas Eve, Jan. 5" The players "claimed to be the 'true and legitimate successors' of the mummers who, in previous centuries, constantly performed at the 'Whitsun' and 'Christmas Church Ales,' records of which are found on almost every page of the Stewards and Churchwardens' Books of the Prebendal Church of our Blessed Lady of Thames." But these records are as vague as those in the Lincolnshire archives.

manuscript of 1685 do we have a connection even as specific as the mention of characters such as St. George and Beelzebub.[1]

This lack of historical detail, however, should not necessarily block our investigation of the field any more than the undocumented gaps have blocked the valuable work that has been done on reconstruction of the Elizabethan theaters. The gaps here can be filled, perhaps more tentatively than one would wish, by analogous continental ceremonies. This is where the extraordinary findings of scholars such as A. J. B. Wace,[23] R. M. Dawkins,[24] and Violet Alford[25] will serve us.

With these basic problems of investigation clearly in mind, then, we shall study the form of the men's ceremonial in the next chapters, examining in turn the physical elements of the performance, the typical Hero-Combat action, the Sword Play, and the Wooing Ceremony.

---

[1] Charles Read Baskerville, "Mummers' Wooing Plays," *MP*, XXI (February 1924), 230, has pointed out one reference to a play that could conceivably be construed as a wooing ceremony in *The Taming of the Shrew*. In the Introduction, the Lord says to the First Player,

> This fellow I remember,
> Since once he played a farmer's eldest son:-
> 'Twas where you wooed the gentlewoman so well:

References from play texts are tenuous at best, no matter how many one piles together and this one, being addressed to a professional strolling player places it at an even further remove from the kind of folk drama we are discussing.

TWO

PERFORMING THE ACTION

Witnessing a performance of the men's dramatic ceremony is an experience radically different from witnessing a literary play. The occasion, the stage, the performers, the costumes, the style of acting, the attitude of the performers toward the text, and the audience are all subject to conventions far removed from those of the realistic proscenium theater. For this reason it is important to be aware of the specific performance elements of the ceremony before looking at the plays themselves.

The Visit

Our awareness of the difference begins with our first desire to see the play. Supposing it is the right time of the year—even further, the right *day* of the year—we do not "go to the play." Perhaps we go to the town where we know a troupe will be out. That is as much as we can do. Then we must wait for the play to come to us.

The visit is inherent in the ceremony's structure. The play is short. It does not usually last more than half an hour, even with the extended *quêtes* we find in the later examples.[A] Most texts clearly point to the action of announcing the arrival of the troupe in a place not designed for dramatic performances. Sometimes specific directions on how to approach

[A] *Quête* is a term used to denote any kind of perambulatory collection. The American children's custom of "trick-or-treating" on Halloween, for instance, could be considered a pure *quête*. In the men's ceremonial this label is generally attached to the final section of the play when money or food is finally openly requested.

a house are given. In the Guilden Sutton Soul-Cakers' Play from Cheshire, for instance, there is a song outside the door. "The Players then knock at your door, you open it for them. One player enters at a time, the others wait outside for their turns." [1] The first player to speak in this case is called Open Doors.[B]

The route of the Antrobus Soul-Cakers for Saturday night, November 15, 1949, affords a good example of the visiting nature of the ceremony today. The Antrobus troupe is considered a traditional one. That is, it is one that has either had no break in the natural flow of the tradition of playing or has been revived with directions from a player or witness from a time before the break.

Sat. 11:15

George and Dragon, Gt. Budworth	7:30
Cock Inn, St. Budworth	8:00
Wheatsheaf Inn, Antrobus	8:30
Brick and Bottle, Whitley	9:00
Chetwode Arms, Whitley	9:30
Dance in Whitley Schools	10:15 [2]

It is obvious from the Antrobus itinerary that by now the chief stops are the pubs. Although it was originally the houses in the area that were the important stopping places, the pub now seems to be the favorite stage of most of the troupes. It is a natural development. As houses in one area become less scattered and more numerous, as the community loses its specifically agricultural identity, and as the *quête* takes on more importance, it is the pub which affords the troupe the largest, most generous audience.

The importance of the *quête* in connection with the visit is given a different focus by Thomas Hardy in his reminiscences of local survivals of ancient customs in William Archer's *Real Conversations*. "Sometimes a large village would furnish forth two sets of mummers," he says. "They would go to the farmhouses round, between Christmas and Twelfth Night doing some four or five performances each evening, and getting ale and money at every house. Sometimes the mummers of one village

---

[B] In another version, from Sapperton, Gloucestershire (n.d.), the words, "Please to let the mummers act," are prefixed to the First Player's speech. R. J. E. Tiddy, *The Mummers' Play* (Oxford, 1923), p. 170.

would encroach on the traditional sphere of influence of another village and then there would be a battle in good earnest."[c] Hardy's memory here shows us that even before the twentieth century the collection was important enough to fight over.

Aside from the importance of the *quête,* however, we can see that there is something deeper underlying the ceremony as a visit or procession. The Marshfield Paper Boys, another traditional troupe, do not move from house to house. They remain outdoors all through the ceremony, moving from station to station in the town. There is an air of mystery about this, particularly since they never announce what all these stations will be beforehand.[3] One member of the English Folk Dance and Song Society once remarked she had been pleased because she had been "tipped off" as to where to stand in Marshfield so that she could get to see the Paper Boys. She would not tell where that place was for fear, she said, that it would "break their luck." This is, of course, a suspiciously excessive attitude, but the theme of excitement and mystery at the arrival of the players is one that threads through all the reminiscences of the play. Whether one is in a pub, the kitchen of a farmhouse, the drawing room of a great house, or on a winter road, he is, like my folklorist friend, anticipating the visit of the troupe, waiting for them to come to him.

In the case of the Marshfield Paper Boys, it is certainly not the *quête* which accounts for the processional nature of the performance. This troupe refuses to collect anything after a performance. The members are strongly aware that they are the ones who have something to dispense— and that thing, in their own words, is "luck."

Margaret Dean-Smith in her article "Folk Play Origins of the English Masque" makes a great deal of the visit as basic to the ceremonial. She believes it is this that connects the court masque directly with the folk drama. She views the original purpose of the masque procession as the bringing of "prosperity and goodwill, either by the act of perambulation with dances or other enactments performed in station,"[4] and sees it as a direct descendant of the luck-bringing ceremonial procession we are discussing here.[5]

---

[c] William Archer, *Real Conversations* (London, 1904), p. 35. Hardy, of course, had already made brilliant use of the men's ceremonial in *The Return of the Native,* Bk. II, ch. V.

The visit, then, is the first element we must keep in mind as an essential of the performance.[D] The next is the stage.

The Stage and the Circle

Since there is no theater building to house this dramatic event, its stage must be created anew with every performance. This is far from a haphazard business in the men's dramatic ceremony. It is the first element to set it apart from other seasonal ceremonies such as the May Procession, the Derby Tup, the Hunting of the Wren and specific hobby-horse processions such as the one at Padstow and the Welsh Mari Llwyd. In all of these, the processional element is present, just as it is in the men's dramatic ceremony. What does not occur in these others is the clear separation between the audience and the actors. It is only in the men's dramatic ceremony that the action is set apart from the spectators yet made accessible to all of them by the drawing of the circle.

How this is accomplished may vary from play to play. In some it may be done by the performers all entering at once and walking around in a circle while they sing or while the Presenter gives his first speech. Once the prologue is finished, the performers may then retire from the room, or more often, pull back and range around the circumference of the circle. This is sometimes dictated by the size of the room. In other cases it may be the Presenter who walks around, declaiming a prologue that calls for "room" and setting the boundaries of the action as he walks. In still others it may be the "female" who comes in with a broom and clears a circle by sweeping the spectators back.

In the Guilden Sutton play, "each player enters separately and walks round in a circle till he gets to the words 'if you don't believe, etc, step

[D] One interesting and rather comic sidelight to this visiting nature of the ceremony is the difficulty it caused in Ireland. It was the processional nature that caused the disbanding of a number of troupes near the Irish border. In a letter from a collector who interviewed a former player we are told, "Mr. De Lacy, the player, reckoned that the Border situation finally killed it. Passes weren't given to troupes of Mummers wanting to traipse back and forth over the Border, and gangs of disguised men roaming round at night were not popular with the Royal Ulster Constabulary." The letter is dated August 18, 1965. H.C., XXII, 226. It is difficult to tell here which confounded the Royal Constabulary more, the disguise or the procession. Whichever it was, the idea of the querulous Constabulary helpless against tradition and finally having to "kill it" is delightfully comic.

in and clear the way.' He then steps aside and ushers in the next player
with a slight movement of his hand till all the actors are assembled." [6]
There are nine characters in this play, including Dick, the hobby-horse,
and his driver, which means that the circle is made nine times before
the action begins.[E]

The call for room constantly recurs in the beginning of the plays.
Although it is not usually directly connected with the forming of the
circle, it is certainly a call for the clearing of the acting area. In a play
collected from Gander, Kentucky, the call for room is specifically associ-
ated with the circle. In this version, originating in England, the Presenter
"sweeps a wide circle all the time muttering over and over, 'Room, room,
gallons of room,'" a corruption of the familiar call of "Room, room,
gallants, room!" He then presents all seven characters who "strut around
the outside of the circle and step out of the circle until their parts. . . ." [7]
There is no doubt that the circle plays a significant part in separating
the action from the audience here, for the only two players who have
direct contact with the spectators remain outside the circle.[F] Bessy and
Bet, when they are not directly related to the drama, "tease the audience,
she pretending to kiss the men, he the women." [8]

The clearing of the circle for the stage can be viewed in a number of
different ways, none of which is mutually exclusive. The first is the
practical; the next is in connection with primitive ritual; still another is
as a specific element of magic in the ceremony.

[E] In Thame, Oxfordshire, all the mummers come in together singing and
form the circle at once. After the song they all stand to one side, but the acting
area is now clear for King Alfred and his Queen to "enter" which means nothing
more than moving into the center of the circle from the circumference. Frederick
George Lee, "Oxfordshire Christmas," *NQ,* 5th s., II (December 26, 1874), 504.
H.C., I, 357.

In Upper and Lower Howsell, Worcestershire, where the play is performed
outdoors, Little Devil Doubt clears a circle by brushing away the snow with
his besom. Cuthbert Bede, "Modern Mumming," *NQ,* 2nd s., XI (April 6, 1861)
271. H.C., VII, 15.

In Kempsford, Gloucestershire, "The audience stood round the side of the
room while the Players occupied the space in the middle, walking round and
round, beating the floor with their staves." Tiddy, p. 249. H.C., I, 53.

[F] Perhaps the most interesting and elaborate examples of the creation of
the circle for the stage occur in the Sword Play Ceremonies. See below, pp. 73–
74 for a description of the Greatham Sword Dance circle. See also Maud Karpeles,
"Some Fragments of Sword Dance Plays," *JEFDS,* 2nd s., II (1928), 35–42.
H.C., I, 26–73.

The performers have no raised stage to separate them from the audience; therefore, the most efficient method of clearing sight lines for as much of the audience as possible is by creating a circular playing area around which the spectators can arrange themselves. It is the most natural shape for this informal kind of performance's stage to take. This is certainly the most sensible, practical view of the reason for the circle as stage.

Arthur H. Beatty and Richard Southern, however, go further, using the circular acting area to relate the play to primitive ritual drama. Southern uses the circle as one criterion to place the play in what he calls the first "age" of the theater. He shows us how the circle evolves as the most primitive solution to the practical problem of sight lines not only in the mummers' play but in the Tibetan festival dramas and the Mexican Flying Festivals.[9] Beatty uses the circular stage as one of the five constant elements in order to draw analogies between the play and Australian Intichiuma ceremony, the Easter celebration of Little Russia, and the American Zuni initiation ceremony.[10]

The view of the circle as an element of magic is somewhat more complicated, but we must begin to deal with it here, since it is in this area that the richness of the implications of the ceremony's survival may be found. This, too, connects with the idea of the primitive nature of the ceremony. It also puts the play in relationship to a number of clearly primitive dances. Violet Alford, in her book *Sword Dance and Drama,* deals with this relationship in terms of the Sword Dance. In trying to trace the origins and meanings in the Sword Dance figures, Miss Alford tells us:

> The simplest figures show the clearest resemblance. The closed chain forming the sunwise (i.e., clockwise) moving circle is invariably used in ritual dances and has been inherited by recreational, social dances. This is *deasil* (from the Celtic). When traced counter-clockwise the Circle is Malificent and is called *widdershins.* It quite simply portrays the sun's track across the heavens and from far distant times has been used to insure that, with this human aid, the sun will follow its appointed course.
>
> The circle is used in every sort of magic-making even today. It keeps in safety whatever is placed inside it; a circle against the power of a malevolent witch may be drawn by a white one, a sick cow led inside while prayers and charms are said over her, or a Bridal pair to protect and fertilize.[11]

This idea of the circle as a place of safety for the Bridal pair will take on particular significance when we look at the all-important Wooing Ceremony and its European counterparts. Alford's analysis of the use of the circle in primitive dance is an extraordinarily packed one, bringing together the ideas of fertility, good and evil, the sun, and safety. All of these are dealt with in the action of the ceremonial, as we shall see when we look closely at individual examples.

It would, of course, be folly to try to infer the magical nature of the ceremony from the single fact that it is performed in a circular area. If this fact stood alone, the only substantial explanation necessary would be the first, practical one. It is when we see it in conjunction with the other features of the performance of the play that the idea of the circle as a magical symbol becomes relevant. As we look at the separate elements one by one, we shall begin to see them informing each other until the concept of magic as an essential, underlying purpose becomes inescapable. We have already seen the element of the visit referred to as a "luck-bringing perambulation"; now we see the circle as a possible signpost to a survival of a more primitive kind of magic. Let us move ahead to the performers and their costumes and see if this element is consistent with the emerging picture.

The Players

The custom of reserving the task of performing the play for men only is one that has endured to the twentieth century. Even in its most decadent form, this exclusiveness still obtains. There is only a handful of traditional troupes still extant. Many modern performances are initiated by schoolmasters for grammar and public school recitations at Christmas and Easter; but even in Midgley, Yorkshire, where a compilation of chapbook versions is performed by schoolchildren, it is only male schoolchildren who participate. The strength of this tradition becomes even clearer when we look at what has happened to other men's ceremonials. The morris, for instance, originally the exclusive province of men, is now being danced by women, too. In Lancashire and Cheshire, there are even women's morris competitions. During the war, because of the scarcity of men, young girls also began performing the individual crossed-sword dance of the Scottish Highlands. That it was originally a strictly male province women have entered here is apparent from the vociferous disapproval of many of the traditionalists in England today. One morris dancer, a fairly moderate and level-headed gentleman, told me, "Oh, I'm quite reasonable about the whole thing. Let them dance all they want." Then he gritted his teeth and added, *"Only not in public."*

The tradition of the dramatic ceremony as a strictly masculine ritual, however, has proved stronger. Thus far, it has thoroughly withstood any feminine assault.[G] We can see a number of reasons for the strength of this survival.

First, we have seen that many of the performances have turned into pub-crawling expeditions in which women are not likely to participate. As the evening wears on, and more and more pubs have shown their generosity, the play tends to become more and more ribald. The men would simply resent the inhibiting influence of a woman. In so many of the plays, too, the "female" plays a key role. The idea of the man dressed up as a woman, whether it originally had ritual significance or not, is certainly a source for broad comedy today. With women performing, that source would be gone.

There is still another reason, though, which cannot be pinned down with such easy logic. This has to do with the concept of the men as the priests, the primitive agents of magic. This concept is not unknown in the twentieth century. R. R. Marrett tells the story of an old mummer in the 1930's who was asked by a German professor at Oxford if women ever take part in the plays. " 'No, sir,' he replied, 'mumming don't be for the likes of them. There be plenty else for them that be flirty-like, but this here mumming be more like parson's work.' "[12]

The Dress

There is a wealth of information available to us about the costumes of the men's ceremonial through eyewitness descriptions and photographs.

[G] The only record we have of women participating is in the Ambleside, Westmoreland, Play. Douglas Kennedy, "Observations on the Sword Dance and Mummers' Play," *JEFDS,* 2nd s., III (1930), 36–37. Here we are told that all the performers are girls. Whatever the validity of this report, it is even more interesting to note that even in the decadent mumming contests of County Wexford, so similar to the Morris competitions of Cheshire and Lancashire, the performers are still strictly male.

In *The Return of the Native,* Thomas Hardy has Eustacia Vye participate in a performance. He uses this to emphasize the character's mannish nature and is well aware of the power of the tradition she is breaking.

It is in this area that we have the most fascinating and illuminating phenomenon of the coexistence of the old and the new.

Let us begin with an example of the most recent development in the costume by examining a photograph of the Minehead, Somerset, mummers, all of whom are "dressed in part," and then move back through time until we find the costume in what I believe to be its most basic form in the dress of a troupe like the Marshfield Paper Boys.

There are seventeen players arranged in three rows in the Minehead photograph (see Figure 8). Although at first it appears that there are two women in the picture, a closer examination reveals that they are both disguised men. At the extreme left we see Father Christmas standing in a fur-trimmed robe, false beard, and wig. He holds a cane. Seated next to him is probably Dame Dorrity, an old "woman" wearing a dark, floor-length dress, a large patterned shawl, and a bonnet that covers her entire head. Although it is not perfectly clear because of her light complexion, she appears to have a full brush mustache. She, too, holds a cane before her. Another "female," probably Queen Susan, sits next to her, even more elaborately costumed with a medieval church-steeple on her head, a close, tightly curled 1920's wig, an Elizabethan bodice, complete with cross-lacing at the bosom and ruff, and a Victorian skirt embroidered down the front with four ruffles at the bottom. A pair of large men's shoes peep out from beneath the skirt. Next to her is a man costumed as King John with tights and an elaborate tunic. The style and period of the tunic is not clear because of his position and the fact that most of it is covered by an imitation sable robe. On his head he wears a crown with a cross on the top of the front. Except for four other characters who represent the Giant, Tom Bowling, Sambo, and the Doctor, all the other players are costumed as warriors from a conglomeration of periods.[13] One is in full medieval armour, at least four are dressed as redcoats, and a few are wearing utterly unidentifiable, though not any the less elaborate, uniforms.

There is little question that this kind of elaborate representational costuming is a "decadence" and that the further away we move from simplicity, the further we are from the traditional experience of the play. Except for the black face of Sambo, which can also be viewed here as dressing in part, there is no attempt to disguise the face. There is, however, one striking aspect of the photograph. All the characters have, without exception, some from of a headdress, from the small wig on

Sambo to the highly elaborate hats resembling tall bishops' mitres decorated with crosses, hearts, and stars on the two warriors framing the group in the back.

In an old photograph of the Overton, Hampshire, mummers we see six players. After viewing the Minehead players, the first thing that strikes us about Overton is the silhouette of the costume. There is absolutely no diversity at all.

The men are apparently wearing their own clothes underneath the costume. Tied around the knees is some kind of shredded material which hangs down to the ankles, covering the lower parts of the trouser legs almost completely. Whether the material is cloth or paper is unclear from the photograph. A solid sleeveless tunic covers the upper portion of their bodies to just below the waist. The headdress is again the most elaborate and striking element of the picture. It is about two feet high or more, something like an inverted paper bag, decorated with strips of paper. The shredded material hangs from the top of the headdress almost completely obliterating the faces. Except for the fact that Father Christmas is carrying a staff, it is impossible to distinguish the character of the individual player. The costume is thoroughly non-representational. It is clearly serving a purpose other than differentiation or identification of any kind.

This effect of anonymity, seen at its simplest in the three tiers of shredded material on the Overton mummers, is what creates the startling and mysterious quality of the Marshfield Paper Boys whose costume Richard Southern compares to the dress of figures like the Bavarian Wild Man and the African medicine man.[14] It is achieved with a mass of shredded paper (often newspaper) which begins at the top of the conical headdress and shoulders and falls all the way down the body until nothing can be distinguished beneath it but a pair of farm boots. The faces are thoroughly indistinguishable.

It is almost impossible to describe the eerie effect that a series of action photographs of a performance in Marshfield has upon the viewer (see Figures 2 and 3). The setting is outdoors. Set in the middle of the street is a circle of figures—one cannot even say men; they are all so utterly formless. In one shot two figures are in the center of the circle, obviously in conflict. There are swords. In another, one of the figures is on the ground. What is brought home in these pictures, more clearly than any text could possibly do, is the utter purity of action in the per-

formance. It would be impossible for a character name to have any meaning in a costume like this. What is being enacted is conflict, pure and
simple, conflict at its most elemental level, stripped to only the most
basic essential: opposing forces.[H]

It is indisputable that the example of "dressing in part" we have seen
in the Minehead mummers is a late sign of the "decadence of the play,"
as Alex Helm calls it,[15] and that Overton and Marshfield represent the
more traditional dress. From Drayton, Buckinghamshire, in fact, we have
two descriptions of the dress of the players, one giving details of the
"ancient" costume and one for a performance of around 1905.[I] The old
costume was made up of the familiar pointed hats with streamers and
strips of paper sewn on to ordinary clothes, while in the modern performance the players were all dressed in part, King George and Bold
Slasher wearing khakis and military tunics.

There is no attempt at realistic representation in any of the traditional examples. Rather, the purpose seems to be one of insisting upon
a total lack of identification and this leads us to what is a consistently
documented purpose of traditional men's ceremonial dress, the simple
purpose of disguise.

Tiddy deals with the importance of disguise and anonymity in his
preface to *The Mummers' Play,* when he says:

[H] E. K. Chambers, p. 84, sees the shredded costume as representing the
scales of the dragon in the legend of St. George. This seems to me untenable
since, as we have seen, St. George is not by any means an essential figure in the
play and even where he does play a part there are only a handful of late,
thoroughly atypical versions in which the dragon appears at all. Besides this,
the most obvious question is, if the costume represents the scales of the dragon,
what is it doing on all the characters?
Another approach holds that it represents a kind of leafy "armour" connecting the qualities of the medieval romance with the "green man" of so many
primitive ceremonies. Beatty, 276. Even here where it is so well argued, I believe too much is being made of the St. George element of the play. The original
costume may have been one of leaves or green branches. But it is an error to
try to view the costume as any kind of representation at all. It would be safer
to view the original use of branches and leaves as likely simply because these
were the most readily available materials for ceremonial dress, just as strips
of paper and rags are the most accessible materials now.
[I] MS. in Vaughan Williams Library Collection (n.d.) H.C., II, 370–377.
There is, unfortunately, no date given for the appearance of the traditional
costume. The term "ancient" was used by the player whom the collector interviewed. The point here, however, is that the non-representational costume
clearly preceded the representational one.

That the identity of the figures should not be clearly known was of the very essence of the early ritual play. The blackened faces, the masks and the mumming were designed with this object, and in the north and in Cornwall the mummers are still actually known as "guizers." When once the characters are intelligibly named, the mystery, the solemnity and the sense of danger, which had induced the performers to disguise themselves, are gone. . . .[16]

In the play from Gander, Kentucky, we have a revival. Many of the spectators were unfamiliar with the tradition of the men's ceremonial. The Presenter's first speech makes the background of the revival clear while it also deals specifically with the need for anonymity on the part of the actors.

We air now aiming to give a dumb show for to please the Little Teacher for not going off to the level country to keep Christmas with her kin. Hit ain't noways perfect the way we act out this here dumb show, but hit ain't been acted out amongst our settlement for upwards of twenty or thirty year, maybe more. I reckon folks all knows hit air bad luck to talk with the dumb show folks or guess who they air. Now then we aim to start.[17]

Although the narrator calls it a "dumb show," the characters are reported to have spoken. Their voices, however, were used unnaturally, giving the words their traditional chanted quality. This alteration of the normal voice may well be another method of disguise.[J] This concept of the disguised voice as well as the disguised face and body may well be a better explanation of the term "mummers" than one which deals only with the connotations of silence which the word carries today.

The importance of disguise also explains the ubiquitous emphasis on elaborate headdress in the men's ceremonial. In Overton and Marshfield we saw that the most important fringe, that which made recognition impossible by hiding the faces of the performers, hung from the headpiece. This is also true of the Symondsbury,[18] Drayton[19] and Shrewton[20] troupes. As we look at a series of headdresses from various troupes, we can see a gradual development following a pattern similar to the one

---

[J] See below, pp. 27–28, for other examples of chanting, intoning and singing. I am grateful to Dr. S. F. Johnson for pointing out the idea of the alteration of voices as another form of disguise.

we will be tracing in the development of the form of the play itself.

We have already seen the headdress with the original primitive purpose of disguise in Marshfield and Overton. As we move forward in time and as disguise no longer comprises an essential element of the ritual, the face covering simplifies and becomes mere decoration. This is the case with the costume for the Hampshire Jolly Jacks, for instance, where no more than two or three strips hang suspended in a vertical arc from the headpiece over the top part of the player's face.

While the concept of disguise has diminished in importance, the development of the headdress split off into two directions. In one, the emphasis is placed on elaborate decoration; in the other it is on representation.

In the first direction, we see the gradual loss of the face covering and the appearance of increasingly complex designs on the head itself. This can be seen specifically in the Netley Abbey mummers of Hampshire who wear non-representational costumes made up of about fifty short tiers of colored material and enormously elaborate, rosetted hats extending two feet over their heads. Their faces are completely uncovered.[K]

In the second direction—toward representation—the initial representation is symbolic. We see this in the Abbots Bromley Horn Dancers in which what seems to be a bizarre headdress of animal horns is not even worn, but carried by each dancer. The faces of the dancers are no longer covered and the horns are carried, not to make us believe that the dancers are impersonating or transformed into the horned animal, but as symbols of fertility. It is only later, with an example like the one we have studied in Minehead, that the concept of fully realistic representation emerges. This movement from non-representational ritual disguise through symbolic interpretation to realistic representation is a pattern similar to Theodor Gaster's tracing of the progression, on a much larger scale, from non-representational magical ritual to symbolic myth [21] and the Cambridge scholars' further tracing of that symbolic myth to the representational Greek drama.[22]

[K] M. W. Barley, "Plough Plays," *JEFDSS,* VII (December 1952), 77, tells of one member of the Alkborough team who wore a stovepipe hat covered with beads and brooches collected solely for their decorative value. By the time the hat was worn, it weighed seven pounds. It was not unusual, either, for hats to be covered with watch chains, coins, and small mirrors as well, and end up with over five pounds sterling worth of jewelry on them.

The Acting Style

The final element to be considered here before going on to discuss the specific forms of the three different kinds of plays is the acting style and, in connection with this, the attitude of the players toward the text and the audience. Here, as in the area of costume, we can see two different stages of tradition coexisting.

Although it is possible that the ceremonial originally had no words to it at all, by the time we have documented records, words are an integral part of the performance. In the records of the performances we have, these words are either treated with almost mystical reverence, no matter how nonsensical they may appear, or they are dealt with simply as skeletal ideas which guide the players to the action and leave them free to improvise as broadly as they please.

The Ripon Sword Play in Yorkshire affords an excellent example of the first kind of approach. Here the six performers stand in a straight line. They speak at the tops of their voices, with absolutely no inflection. When the man whom the Doctor refers to as "Jack" is killed, he simply drops his head. One of the players calls for the doctor and puts his hand on Jack's shoulder. He keeps it there until the revival.[23] It is interesting that along with this thoroughly ritualistic, non-representational approach to the performing of the action, little attention is paid to specific character names or even to which of the combatants is killed. The text is always referred to simply as "The Words of the Ripon Sword Dance." [24]

It is this kind of approach to the acting of the play that Thomas Hardy recalls when he describes a performance of the Hero-Combat from his childhood.

> Rude as it was, the thing used to impress me very much—I can clearly recall the odd sort of thrill it would give. The performers used to carry a long staff in one hand and a wooden sword in the other and pace monotonously around, intoning their parts on one note, and punctuating them by nicking the sword against the staff—something like this: "Here come I, the Valiant Soldier (*nick*), Slasher is my name (*nick*)." [25]

This sounds almost exactly like the record we have of the Chithurst, Sussex, Tipteerer's Play in which we are told:

*The Turkish Knight retires, and the Noble Captain and the Doctor come forward to the middle of the stage, and sing, crossing and hitting their swords at the words following ***

NOBLE CAPTAIN
I * am the blade
DR. GOOD
That * drives no trade,
BOTH
Most * people * do * adore * me.
I * will you * beat, and I * won't you * cheat,
And I'll * drive you * all * before me.

This continues for ten more lines:

Then follows a dialogue between the doctor and all the rest, who chant the answer in chorus . . .[L]

Alex Helm stated that this bald, declamatory style has become traditional simply because the performers are untrained actors and unable to give sense to their lines.[M] This would be reasonable if "sense" were what is important in the words, but here is where Helm fell into the trap he was so careful to avoid in all other areas of his study of the play. He approached it as a play rather than the survival of a ritual action.

One of the major distinctions between the literary play and the ritual lies in the attitude of the performers toward the words and the audience. In the ritual an action is performed as imitation or magic. The spectators watch, but the players are not communicating directly with them. If the spectator partakes of the action itself, he is no longer a spectator; he is a performer, too. In the performance of the action, voices and bodies are used to effect whatever it is that is the object of the ritual, whether it be fertility for the land, prosperity for the tribe, health for the body, or grace for the soul. An audience is ultimately no necessity. The ritual would be performed whether there were spectators present or not.

In the drama, however, the action is no longer self-contained. The

[L] H.C., VI, 126–132. See above, p. 25n.
[M] Helm, "In Comes I," 128. He later informed me that his thoughts on this changed considerably.

players communicate directly with the audience. The focus is now on *explaining* the action to the audience. This is where the word "sense" becomes important in the way Helm approaches it.

The ritual is pure action and when dealing with it we can only describe what happens and its purpose. We cannot deal with how it is made meaningful in any way to the audience for it is not designed to be made meaningful to an audience at all.

Now, the men's ceremonial as we have it today has already evolved into drama. When a character moves into the middle of the circle, crying

> In comes I, King George,
> King George that valiant man with courage bold,
> 'Twas I that won five crowns of gold.
> 'Twas I that fought the fiery dragon and brought him to a slaughter,
> And by that fight I hope to win the Queen of Egypt's daughter,[26]

he is surrounding the basic combat with words that will allow it to make sense to an audience. But the large number of verbal variants that surround the action in all the texts must inevitably lead us to the conclusion that it was not the meaning of the action as expressed in the words that was originally the important feature.

All the elements of the performance we have looked at so far such as the visit, the circle, and the disguise, as well as its seasonal appearance, lead us to believe it was simply the ritual performance of the action that was its *raison d' être,* and that if there were words attached, they were used to effect a result within the context of the action itself and not to serve an interpretative role for an unnecessary audience.

It is this distinction that weakens the theory that the reason for the declamatory, inflectionless delivery of the words is due to the player's inability to make "sense" out of them. It is, rather, that the declamatory, intoning method is traditional because it is an integral part of what was originally pure ritual action in which the words (or whatever accompanying sounds they might originally have been) serve an effective, magical purpose, not an affective, communicative one.

There is still, however, the second style of acting that also must be considered. This is the improvisational style.

The text of the Chadlington, Oxfordshire, play, recorded in 1893, suddenly breaks off when it reaches the dialogue between Jack Finney and the Doctor. It is not recordable, we are told, because it was thoroughly improvised and "varied according to the class of the audience." All the collector tells us is: "They wrangle in this way. At last they belabour the fallen King George with a bladder at the end of a stick. This is the great point from the rustics' point of view."[27] This kind of record is not unusual in the collections of the plays.[N]

The improvisatory style seems, at first, to be thoroughly incompatible with the declamatory ritual style. On closer examination, however, we find they have one thing in common. Both tend to minimize the importance of the words in favor of the action. The intoning of the words sacrifices literal "sense" to efficacy; improvisation subordinates the importance of the words to the burlesque action they surround. It is not unusual to find both styles mixed in one performance, with the sections directly related to the combat delivered in the formal, chanting style. It is generally with the appearance of the doctor that the style changes and the improvised fun begins.

The Crookham play is one example of this mixture. The appearance of the players is preceded by a knocking at the door and the words, "Please kind master and mistress may we come in and say our play."

[N] In 1949, Mr. Collins, the leader of the Antrobus troupe, told Alex Helm that there were two versions of the play—"one performed when there are ladies present and another one for exclusive male company in public houses." H.C., I, 7–8.

One of the most complete records of his kind of improvisatory approach is a letter from Roy Dommett in 1965 describing the performance of the Crookham play.

> Opportunities for interpolating remarks about or at persons or things present at a performance were never missed. The Turkish knight / King George [sic] bit brought remarks about UDI and Rhodesia from the rest of the men.
> . . . the doctor . . . unloaded his bag with such things as a chopper-"scalpel," string-"suture," mallet-"anaesthetic." He waved the chopper over the bodies as if to slit them down the middle which made the corpses squirm. With a pair of pliers or cutters he made as if to pull teeth or trim their noses. He would wave his bottle—a very large medicine bottle—saying "you can't get this on the National Health." [H.C., XXIII, 53].

It is interesting to note that even in Antrobus where the words seem not at all important there is a mystique about them. In the note quoted above, Helm goes on to say that the gang was reluctant to commit the play to paper. One gentleman had been refused the script the year before and although Collins was willing to give it to Helm, the rest of the gang refused.

The players file in, led by the musician. They walk around the arena two or three times and fall out into two facing lines from which they step forward and say their pieces. The opening speeches are delivered out of a set routine. The communicant of the play tells us that King George marches to and fro during his speeches, "each length being about two lines worth. His challengers countermarch with him and they cross swords at each passing." When Bold Roamer and Bold Slasher are dead, they lie on their backs.

After this, the quality changes. The Doctor arrives with a black bag filled with tools and a large bottle and small phial. He cures the men who wriggle and come to life when they are told to get up. Then follows a burlesque combat between Johnny Jack and Father Christmas. The text recorded in 1964 is indicative of the change in tone that occurs here. The early challenges between King George and Bold Slasher are the conventional ones.

> BOLD ROAMER: Oh, yes, King George there is a man stands in this room
> That you can't cut down under your created hand.
> So battle to battle you and I must play, to see who on this ground shall lay.
> KING GEORGE: So battle to battle you and I must play, to see who on this ground shall lay
> So mind your hits and guard your blows, likewise your head and your eyes also.[28]

But the horseplay between Father Christmas and Johnny Jack smacks of music hall gags, although their incomprehensibility leads us to believe that it is the accompanying comic action that is important.

> FATHER CHRISTMAS: So you think you are the best man of all.
> JOHNNY JACK: Yes I do.
> FATHER CHRISTMAS: I knew your father years ago.
> JOHNNY JACK: I never had one!
> FATHER CHRISTMAS: Oh yes you did! I bought pigs off him.
> JOHNNY JACK: Never kept any.
> FATHER CHRISTMAS: I kept them pigs in the straw yard and they died for want of a litter. So you think you're the best man of all?
> JOHNNY JACK: Yes, I do.

FATHER CHRISTMAS: So you do, do you! I think I will have a go
with you.
(*They fight. Father Christmas defending himself with his broom held
in both hands horizontally. Father Christmas is killed.*) [29]

We are also told that, in contrast to the deaths of the hero-combatants,
Father Christmas dies on his stomach and Johnny Jack sits on him.[30]

These, then, are the basic elements of the performance which we must
keep before us as we examine the textual information on the three
types of ceremony. The performance is a purposeful visit; it is performed
in a circular playing area which is newly made with each performance;
the players are male; they are traditionally costumed to disguise their
identities rather than create a representational illusion; and, finally, they
chant or improvise the words which always play a subordinate role to
the action being played out.

After we have dealt more fully with the history and development of
the ceremony and considered it in the light of analagous continental
customs, we shall see that it is, indeed, precisely what the accumulated
evidence of these performance elements implies; an event that began as
pure ritual, with all the magical, effective purposes that word denotes,
whose development began with the separation of performer and audience and the need to explain the action, but whose growth was somehow arrested before it reached the final stage of the fully realized artistic
form of literate drama.

Figure 1. A Marshfield Paper Boy: Costume as Disguise.
The player wears strips of paper over his street clothes. Only the sceptre
and orb tell us that he is "King William."

Figure 2. The Marshfield Paper Boys: The Stage as Circle
The Marshfield troupe performs outdoors. The wounded man inside the
circle of players awaits treatment from the "doctor."

Figure 3. The Marshfield Paper Boys: The Play as an Action.
"King William" and "Little John" in a combat action at the East Gate
of the village outside the old Almshouse. The troupe follows the village
crier to the different stations of the town.

Figure 4. Morris Dancing at Bampton: The Dance as Community Action. Members of the Morris side wear bowler hats with a nosegay of flowers and brightly colored streamers. When he feels like it, the "all-licensed" Fool belabours the dancers with his bladder and cries, "Come on, you lazy lot of rascals!"

Figure 5. The Horn Dance.

The dancers travel some twenty miles over Abbots Bromley, visiting farms and Blithfield Hall every first Monday after September 4. They perform no play.

Figure 6. A Horn Dancer.
The reindeer antlers weigh up to 25 pounds each. The men carry them mounted on a stick. James Fowell, the leader, aged 60, started as the boy playing the triangle. He worked his way up through Bowman, Hobby Horse, and the lesser dancers.

Figure 7. The Abbots Bromley Horn Dancers: The Hobby Horse.
This kind of "animal disguise" also appears in the dramatic ceremonial. This
horse's mouth moves by pulling the string. The Fool carries a bladder on
a stick.

Figure 8. The Minehead Mummers: Dressing in Part.
Even the representational costumes are worn over street clothes. The boots
of the "females" peep out underneath their skirts. Hats or wigs are essential
to the "disguise."

Figure 9. The Goathland Plough Stots: The Play as a Visit.
The plough stots travel from farm to farm, performing their play and
dispensing good luck. The strips of colored cloth on their clothes are
remnants of the old disguise.

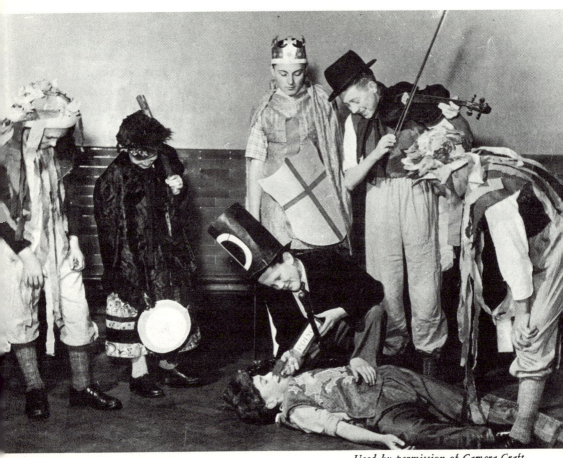

Figure 10. The Darlston Folk Play: A Children's Performance.
Many of these plays are now performed by schoolboys at the Christmas
season. In this performance the old and new kinds of costume are represented.

Figure 11. The Midgley Pace Egg Play.
A Hero-Combat performed at Easter by the schoolchildren of Midgley.
Note the elaborate headdress and the remnant of disguise in the paper
rosettes on the tunics.

Figure 12. Grenoside Sword Dancers: The Lock.
The five dancers form a lock with their swords and place it over the head
of their captain. When the rabbit fur hat is knocked off, the captain falls.
A splendid example of the communal symbolic slaying.

Figure 13. The Bampton Mumming Play: The Doctor.
The Bampton play is always performed in the village pubs. It includes some
of the most inventive improvisatory comedy of the plays that are still
performed. Note the doctor's top hat and frock coat as well as the
representational disguise of mustache and beard.

THREE

THE HERO-COMBAT

It is now time to look closely at the three types of ceremony.

The first and most widespread type is the Hero-Combat. Although, as we have said, it is only the combat, the death, and the resurrection which are the constant elements in all these plays, it would be profitable to examine one representative text containing other fairly common elements, discuss them, and then deal with other variations as well as some of the thoroughly atypical examples which have come to light since Chambers' book.

The Netley Abbey Mummers' Play—A Representative Text

The Netley Abbey Mummers' Play begins with a character called First Christmas Boy, who has a short, introductory speech and calls in Father Christmas. Father Christmas introduces himself with four lines which we find recurring over and over in the Christmas versions of the play.

> In comes I, old Father Christmas
> Welcome or welcome not,
> I hope old Father Christmas
> Will never be forgot.[A]

He calls for room, introduces King George "and all his noble train," and promises "a most dreadful battle that ever was known." King

---

[A] Netley Abbey, Hampshire. S. Peppler, Esq., MS., January 9, 1893, Ordish Collection. H.C., V, 120–123. All direct quotations from this play are from H.C. The complete text is reproduced in Appendix A.

46

George enters and gives a short history of himself, including his winning of "five crowns of gold," his slaying of the dragon, and his love of the "Queen of Egypt's daughter." The Turkey Snipe, a corruption of Turkish Knight, enters and challenges King George. There follows an exchange of challenges between the two. This leads directly to the combat in which King George kills the Turkey Snipe. Immediately afterward, King George boasts to the spectators and then, quite inexplicably, calls for a doctor to cure the Turk. The Doctor appears and proceeds to boast of his cures and his travels. King George and the Doctor agree on a fee for his services and the Doctor cures the Turkey Snipe with two drops of "Oakham, smokum, altigum pain." The Turkey Snipe rises and a procession of unrelated characters follows. The first is Beelzebub, then Poor and Mean, Glutton, Scotch and Scars, Fat and Fine, Jack John, Sweep, Twing Twang, and Tipton Slasher. Each delivers a short, rhymed speech. Johnny Jack, the last figure, asks the audience to

> Give the Christmas Boys what you please.
> A jug of your Christmas ale will make us all merry and sing
> Money in my Christmas box is a very fine thing.

The play can be divided into four major sections. The first three are fairly clear. They are the Introduction, the Combat, and the Cure. Most scholars of the play call the final section the *quête*. The word *"quête"* carries the connotation of a collection, but the final section of the men's ceremonial generally contains more than just a simple collection. In Netley Abbey, for instance, the procession of characters across the stage resembles more a pageant than a collection. This should be kept in mind when we look at the final section of the play.

The Combat

The Combat and the Cure are the dramatic heart of the ceremony and we see in the Netley Abbey text a typical shift in tone between the two. In a majority of the Hero-Combat texts the combat is formally organized with its boasts, challenges, counter-challenges, and final hand-to-hand clash. It is a tone that demands formal presentation. With the appearance of the Doctor, however, the text points to broad comedy and improvisation.

The Combat generally begins with a boast similar to the Netley Abbey

King George's. It tells of the slaying of the dragon, the winning of the hand of the King or Queen's daughter, the winning of the crowns of gold, and, occasionally, the slaying of the Giant Turpin as well.

It is this passage which has led many scholars to assume that the entire Hero-Combat is simply a corruption of an earlier literary work dealing with the dragon theme and George's rescue of Sabra. Richard Johnson's famous *Historie of the Savern* [*sic*] *Champions of Christendom,* 1596, is the work most often cited.[B] But Johnson's work is enormously difficult literature, too difficult in its original form to have captured the imagination of the folk.

The major argument against Johnson, however, or any earlier play as a source for the Hero-Combat lies in the ceremony itself. The Hero-Combat is not about the dragon or the rescue of Sabra at all. These familiar, legendary elements appear in George's first speech and then simply disappear in the ensuing action. The entire play could not possibly take its text or its structure from any of the earlier works which concentrate on Sabra and the dragon.

Besides this, there seems to be no clear pattern or real interest in who is the victor and who the conquered. George falls as often as the Turkish Knight, and in Islip, Oxfordshire, the text even reads, "Instructions: (Decide which is to be dead man and make a good fight.)"[1]

It is possible that the opening lines were taken from some chapbook

<hr>

[B] E. K. Chambers, *The English Folk Play* (Oxford, 1933), pp. 175–177, cites Johnson as a possible source. Johnson's prose romance was adapted for the stage by John Kirke in 1638. See John Kirke, "The Seven Champions of Christendom," ed. G. Dawson, *WRUB,* n.s. XXXII (September 15, 1929), xxiii–xxxix.

Margaret Dean-Smith, "A Note on The Seven Champions," *JEFDSS,* VII (December 1954), 180–181, justly dismisses these works as sources. "It is frankly impossible to see any connection whatever, except that which might be traced to common sources purveyed to the simple in a form more readily understood, remembered and repeated."

A. W. Pollard, *English Miracle Plays* (Oxford, 1895), p. lix, n.2, assumes, on the other hand, that the Hero-Combat is the remains of a lost medieval mystery play of St. George. Although the figure of St. George himself may have found his way into the ceremony through the Christian drama, I believe it is a distortion to assume that the Hero-Combat is a direct outgrowth of the medieval mystery. This assumption of a direct relationship was prevalent in the nineteenth century before the discovery of the many primitive ceremonies on the continent, ceremonies which are directly analagous to the men's ceremonial.

account of St. George, but the sources are not important here. Even if the direct source were to be found, what we would then have would be a literary source for one speech, usually of no more than six to ten lines, out of the entire ceremony. What is of particular interest is that the familiar elements of the St. George story are *previous conquests* which are used at the basis for an opening boast that will lead, finally, to a man-to-man combat. The significance of this will, I believe, become more apparent after we have looked at the remaining combat elements.

Following the boast comes the arrival of the antagonist who is often referred to as the Turkish Knight or some corruption similar to the one in Netley Abbey. He arrives with a counter-boast or an announcement of his desire to fight the protagonist which leads to a direct challenge, answered by a counter-challenge. The antagonists square off and the direct combat begins.[c]

The Netley Abbey play affords a good example of the typical, simple but complete pre-combat action.

Enter King George
   In comes I, King George,
   King George that valiant man with courage bold,
   'Twas I that won five crowns of gold.   BOAST
   'Twas I that fought the fiery dragon and brought him to a slaughter,
   And by that fight I hope to win the Queen of Egypt's daughter.

Turkey Snipe
   In comes I, Turkey Snipe,
   Just come from Turkey Land old England for to fight.
   I'll fight thee King Jarge that valent man,   BOAST
   That valent man of courage bold,
   Let the blood be ever so hot
   I'll shortly draw it cold.

King George
   Ah! ha! my little man
   You talks brave and bold,

[c] These divisions of the protagonists's boast, antagonist's boast, challenge, and counter-challenge are not present in every play. All the fullest texts have them and whenever there is any extended sequence before the direct combat it invariably follows this pattern. Even in examples where the action before the combat is negligible, the fragment that does appear is one that also appears elsewhere in the fully developed form.

Just like some of these little lads I've been told
Pull out your purse and pay,   CHALLENGE
Pull out your sword and fight.
Satisfaction I will have
Before I leave this night.

Turkey Snipe

No purse will I pull out,
No money will I pay,
But my sword I will draw out   COUNTER-CHALLENGE
And have satisfaction of thee this day.
Battle, battle, battle I will call,
And see which on the ground shall fall.

King George

Battle, battle, I will cry,
To see which on the ground shall lie.

Often the combat is stopped midway for another exchange in which the Turk either begs for mercy, which St. George denies him, or the two characters simply present new challenges. This occurs in most of the chapbook versions.[D]

If the words are not important here, the structure of the action is. It is this basic structure of boast, defiance, combat, occasional second defiance, combat, and victory boast which is derivative.

[D] We have an example of this in the play from Burghclere, Hampshire. R. J. E. Tiddy, *The Mummers' Play* (Oxford, 1923), p. 816. After a rather full exchange of challenges, ending with the lines,

King George. Battle to battle with thee
I call to see who on this ground shall fall.
Turkish Knight. Battle to battle with thee
I pray to see who on this ground shall lay.

the description continues,

King George and the Turkish Knight fight and Turkish Knight goes down on one knee and begs pardon.
Turkish Knight. Pardon O Pardon me I crave
an I will be thy Turkish slave.
King George. I neve didn't pardon a Turkish
Knight therefore rise and fight thy might.
Turkish Knight. Battle to battle &c.
King George. Battle to battle &c.
Turkish Knight is wounded and falls.

Dorothy Sayers, in her introduction to *The Song of Roland,* outlines the eleventh century chivalric Rules of Battle beginning with the Defiance followed by the Encounter, the Summons to Surrender, the Death Blow, and the Victor's Boast.[2]

Glynn Wickham traces the development of medieval Battle Training into the Tournament with its highly formal combat of troops, and the development of the Tournament into the Joust between individual combatants.[3] By the time the individual joust was popular, it took its structure from the Arthurian romance. Through all these changes, there remained the basic structure of heraldic boast or sometimes historical exposition, challenge, combat, and victory celebration. As the tournament developed into the joust, Wickham says, "in the process of formation, a species of mimed heroic drama, the central action of which was the actual drama.[4]

Wickham also offers evidence that the common people could and did attend the courtly tournaments of the fifteenth and sixteenth centuries.[E] A popular folk imitation of the tournament, in fact, was the tilt at the Quintain. The Quintain was originally nothing more than some natural tilting target like a tree-trunk or post. But Wickham traces the development of this popular sport into the carving of the target into the resemblance of a human figure until that figure reaches a point most pertinent to our discussion; for the Crusades, of course, "gave to this figure the likeness of a Turk or Saracen, fully armed with a shield on its left arm and a club to brandish with its right." [5] This is exactly the stereotyped figure of the antagonist of the Hero-Combat which comes down to us from the Crusades and is reproduced in the illustrations of the mummers' chapbooks.

It is my belief that the formal structure of the medieval joust and tournament was taken by the folk and grafted on to the basic Men's Ceremonial. This may account for the wide geographical spread of this particular type of play, for it was based on a structure that had not only captured the imagination of the people but was supported, reinforced, and widely dispersed by chapbook accounts.

[E] Wickham, p. 77. A description of the tournament celebrating Katharine of Aragon's marriage to Prince Arthur in 1501 tells of a gallery set off for "the honest and common people." Wickham goes on to say, "The arrangements for accommodating spectators make it clear that opportunity enough existed for Tournaments to colour the popular mind despite the bar against participating as combatants."

It also places the knightly St. George and his crusade-like battle with the Turkish Knight in its proper perspective against the whole of the ceremony. It is an accretion which often colors less than one quarter of the entire performance. Finally, it helps to account for the difference between the early, highly structured quality of the action and the later, improvisational comedy that is introduced with the cure.[F]

The Lament

Often connecting the Combat with the Cure is a short lament for the fallen victim followed by the call for a doctor. The character who has introduced the play, often Father Christmas, is the common mourner. He runs forward, as in the Longborough, Gloucestershire, play, and cries some version of

> Horrible, terrible, what hast thou done?
> Thou has killed my only dearly beloved son
> Is there a doctor to be found
> To cure him of his deep and deadly wound? [6]

If, as in Netley Abbey, there is no Lament, it is usually the victor who calls for the doctor.

The important thing to note here is that when there is a Lament, the mourner invariably identifies the victim as his "son." This is significant, particularly since this Lament is not unique to the Hero-Combat. Some form of it is found in the Wooing Ceremony and the Sword Play, and I believe it is another clue to one of the ritual themes present in the ceremony.

The connection between the lamenter and the lamented is that between age and youth, the relationship that the Presenter commonly promises when he first introduces the play with phrases like

> I'm come to show activity
> This merry Xmastide,
> Activity of youth, activity of age.[G]

[F] It might also be pointed out here that this peculiar split between an early, formal *agon* and later, apparently looser form finds a direct analogy in the structure of Aristophanic comedy that has puzzled so many scholars. See F. M. Cornford, *The Origin of Attic Comedy* (Garden City, 1961), *passim*.

[G] Ilmington, Worcestershire. J. H. Bloom, *Folklore* (London, 1929), p. 113. This is also the thesis of Margaret Dean-Smith, "The Life Cycle," *FL,* LXIX

It should also be noted that a verbal figure most often found in the *quête* is occasionally transferred to the Lament. This is the folk description of the loss of eleven or twelve sons.

> Out of children eleven I've got but seven,
> And they be started up to heaven
> Out of the 7 I've got but 5,
> And they be starved to death alive;
> Out of the five I've got but 3,
> And they be popped behind a tree;
> Out of the 3 I've got but 1,
> And he got around behind the sun.[II]

Now, although I have already pointed out the dangers of using the words of the text for evidence, particularly in trying to make representational sense out of the play, this folk figure of the diminishing "sons" is very likely connected with the loss of the months of the year.

There is a possibility, too, that the word "son," itself, is an unconscious pun, or perhaps even an inadvertent corruption. Certainly one of the themes of this combat is the ritual imitation of the death of the sun in winter and its rebirth in spring. There are versions, too, in which the victor compares the death of the antagonist to the dying of the sun. In Cocking, Sussex, for instance, this not uncommon figure is found in St. George's boast to Father Christmas:

> Oh, Father, Oh father, you see what I've done,
> I've cut this young man down, like the
> evening sun.[I]

(1958), 237–253, when she deals with the folk drama as the playing out of the life cycle, although she deals specifically with the Wooing Ceremony which contains not only Old Age and Youth, but Infancy as well.

[II] Tiddy, p. 178. In the "Johnny Jacks Play" of Overton, Hampshire, as well as in other versions, a fragment of this appears as the lament in the form of Father Christmas crying, "Out of 11 sons I've only got 1 left." In Overton, this occurs after a multiple combat in which Father Christmas claims both antagonists as his sons.

[I] Tiddy, p. 201. In the Whitley, Berkshire, manuscript, reported to have been acted by three generations of the Poulter family and still acted in 1930, we are told that the play had always been transmitted orally. When Twing Twang kills Father Christmas, he sits on his knee and says,

The lament as the transition between the combat and the cure is also an important analagous link between the men's ceremonial and the primitive rituals of Europe. It is, in fact suspiciously like the *Threnos* (Lamentation) preceding the *Anagnorisis* (Discovery and Recognition) and the *Theophany* (Resurrection or Apotheosis) of the Greek ritual form.[7]

E. H. Binney connects the Lament and call for a doctor with a similar structure in the choral *Threnos* of *Alcestis*. In *"The Alcestis* as Folk Drama," Binney gives a description of the Hero-Combat and calls it one of many analagous Death and Revival ceremonies. "Now the myth of Alcestis," he continues,

> represents just such a death and revival; and a myth is so often simply the explanation of a rite that has become unintelligible that one is tempted to conceive that something like our Mummers' play may lie at the bottom of Alcestis. If so the rite would probably survive, if not in the official religion, still in outlying country districts, much as our Mummers' play has survived alongside of and unnoticed by the regular drama. The various characters would have been stereotyped and although there is no need to suppose that Euripides deliberately put a popular mummers' play into literary form when he wrote the Alcestis, still in dramatising the myth he may have consciously or unconsciously reproduced the various characters in their conventional aspect.[8]

He uses this theory to explain some of the peculiarities of the *Alcestis,* such as the happy ending and the burlesque Heracles whom he equates with the burlesque doctor of the mummers' play. For supporting evidence, he also uses the Choral Lament and call for a doctor, which he believes are analagous in the two forms [9] (see Appendix F).

It is important to note the word "analagous" in this discussion, particularly when we relate our ideas to the origins of the Greek drama. It would be absurd to claim a direct relationship between the roots of the Greek drama and the men's ceremonial. We can, however, try to show how the roots of the men's ceremonial lie in a ritual which takes some

---

Hold, behold, look what I've been
  and done.
I've killed my father Abraham
And here sets his son.

But in red ink in the margin are the words, "(Or sun?)." Stuart Piggott, "Mummers' Plays from Berkshire," *FL,* XXXIX (1928), 273. H.C., I. 310.

common shape in many primitive societies and which is most clearly documented in the studies of the origins of Attic tragedy and comedy by scholars like Murray, Binney, Cornford, and Harrison.

The Cure

With the Cure we come to some of the most inventive folk comedy to be found anywhere in the men's ceremonial. We have discussed the improvisational nature of the cure, but even though practically anything can happen in the playing of the cure, when one looks at the recordings of the performances, a formality of structure begins to emerge even here. This consists of the doctor's boast in which he tells of his travels and his powers, a haggle over fees, the administration of the cure, and the resurrection.

In every version, the doctor is treated as the most farcical character of the play. He is inevitably a quack by implication, but in some versions he even refers to himself as "The best quack doctor in the town." [J] His boast, both of travels and cures, follows the same lines as the stock boasts of Renaissance mountebanks.[K] In the Hero-Combat, it is almost always similar to the one we see in Netley Abbey.

> I can cure all diseases;
> I can cure the hitch, the stitch, the palsy and
>   the gout,
> Raging pain both inside and out.
> If the devil's a man, I'll fetch him out.
> Give me an old woman four score and ten,
> With scarcely a stump of tooth in her head,
> I will make her young and plump again.

[J] M. W. Myres, "The Frodsham Soul-Caking Play," FL, XLIII (1932), 99.
In Comberbach, Cheshire, he even uses a familiar type of comic folk inversion, with "the best Doc Quackter you may bet." Arnold Boyd, "The Comberbach Version," TLCA, XLIV (1927), 51. H.C., I, 54.

[K] This is parodied by Ben Jonson in Act II of Volpone. Jonson turns it into great comic literature when Volpone, disguised as Scotus Mantuano, reels off his list of cures. Later, he alludes to the familiar travel boast, so important to the status of the doctor and even includes some internal fee haggling and a history of wonders that invariably accompany the mountebank speech. The Works of Ben Jonson, ed. C. H. Herford and Percy Simpson, V (Oxford, 1937), 53.

More than this. If she falls downstairs and
  breaks her neck,
I will settle and charge nothing for my fees.
Recollect I am not like one of those bony back
  doctors
Who runs about from door to door telling a pack
  of lies,
I will shortly raise the dead before your eyes.

Tiddy has noted the similarity between the boast, with its ubiquitous, rhythmic "itch, stitch, palsy and gout," and the lines reproducing the usual quack boast found in a small, undated volume entitled, *The Harangues, or Speeches of several celebrated quack doctors in Town and Country,* in which a quack boasts he can cure all ills:

Past, present and to come;
  The cramp, the Stitch,
  The squirt, the Itch,
The Gout, the Stone, The Pox,
  the Mulligrubs,
  The Bonny Scrubs
And all Pandora's box.[10]

These boasts are commonplaces, not peculiar to the men's ceremonial, although the doctor, himself, as the agent of the cure, does belong to the basic structure of the action. The specific verbal figures used in the boast as we have them today, are grafted on. The question is, to what have they been grafted?

Felix Grendon, in his study of Anglo-Saxon Charms, gives us the "distinct characteristics which severally appear in a number of the charms." [11] Among others, he cites a Narrative Introduction, the Writing Pronouncing of Patent Names or Letters, Methods of Dealing with Disease Demons, the Exorcist's Boast of Power and Ceremonial Directions to Patient and Exorcist.[12] These ancient elements of magic could easily account for some of the more incomprehensible cures which appear in otherwise fairly coherent versions of the play.

I do not claim that the words here are corruptions of the old Anglo-Saxon charms. That would be impossible to substantiate. What I do believe, however, is that the action of the cure takes its shape from the sequence which Grendon gives us, and which, he says, is common to all Indo-European cultures.[L]

If viewed in this light, the Narrative Introduction becomes the basis for such familiar nonsense figures as the cure of the old man who was dead ninety-nine years and everytime he turned over his bagpipes blew, and

> old Mrs. Cork
> Who had tumbled upstairs
> With an empty teapot full of gin
> She grazed her shins and made her stockings
> bleed.[13]

The Pronouncing of Patent Names and Letters becomes gibberish like "hipigo, limpigo and no go at all," [14] and such gibberish enumeration of the doctor's drugs as:

> Easy peasy peas midget oil and humble
>   bees gravy
> the juice of the beetle, the sap of the
>   pan.
> Three turkey eggs nine miles long
> Put all that together in a midge's bladder
> Stir up with a gray cat's feather.[15]

The clearest connection, of course, is between the boast of the men's ceremonial doctor and the Anglo-Saxon exorcist's boast of power. All of the elements we have examined above can, finally, be subsumed under the heading of the magical boast and it is in this comic action that we see the remains of the once-serious conjurer, exorciser, magical life restorer.[M]

Tiddy, once again, gives us a most sensible account of the doctor's

[L] Grendon, p. 111.
Charles Read Baskerville, "Dramatic Aspects of Medieval Folk Festivals," *SP*, XVII (1920), 28, says, The charms remain our fullest record of the paganism of England. . . . They represent only the magic of pagan religion to the virtual exclusion of those phases of group worship such as the procession, dance and feast out of which most folk drama grew. Yet the charms apparently illustrate the vogue of song in pagan rites and in a few cases—notably in that of the charm for plowed land—the elaboration of mimesis."
[M] There are innumerable continental analogies for this development of the doctor as life-restorer to the stock quack in the death and resurrection ritual. Violet Alford (*Introduction to English Folklore* [London, 1952], p. 28) gives

gradual change from primitive, potent medicine man into the farce character of the present-day play. "The medicine man of savage races is hated so long as he is feared," he suggests. "And his natural or inevitable fate is to become a target for witticisms as soon as that fear is no longer felt." [16]

The cure itself is usually effected with a few drops of Elecampane (or some corruption of that word), an aromatic root once used as a tonic drug in folk medicine. Sometimes it is another kind of wonder medicine applied to the lips, the heart or the temples. Often it is applied to the knee.[x] This is usually accompanied with directions such as

> One drop on the titch bone of his heart
> and one drop on the small of his arm.[17]

This is reminiscent of Grendon's last characteristic of the Anglo-Saxon charm, the Directions to Patient and Exorcist.[o]

There are two atypical cures which should be noted here. In Symonds-

---

us an example of the doctor of the Pyrenean Bear Hunt whose stock speech is a travel boast precisely like that of the Men's Ceremonial doctor. The Pyrenean doctor also connects the ritual and his role directly to the theme of fertility. The Pyrenean Bear Hunt takes place at Gédre, where a man-bear is hunted, killed, and resurrected. During the action, the doctor approaches a couple "to offer Crème Simon for the children. If he is told there are no children, he puts a hand in his medical case and brings out a bean to remedy the lack."

[x] Richard Broxton Onians, *The Origins of European Thought* (Cambridge, 1954), pp. 174–187, discusses the significance of the knee in connection with fertility and birth, citing evidence of belief in the knee as a generative agent in places as diverse as Greece, Rome, Assyria, Babylonia, and Finland. This concept has direct relevance to our study of the roots of the men's ceremonial in fertility ritual. See also below, p. 59 for a discussion of the Bellerby cure; and see p. 92 for an example of more elaborate comic play centered around the knee.

[o] In many versions of the play a tooth-drawing also occurs. In Scrubwood, Buckinghamshire, it takes the place of medicine as a cure. John Bennell and Christopher Wege, MS. (n.d.). H.C. XIX, 589–590.

In Brill, Buckinghamshire, it is an additional element along with shaving. H. Harman, *Sketches of the Buckinghamshire Countryside* (London, 1934), p. 190. H.C., V. 5.

Even more significant is the action from Bearstall, Buckinghamshire, in which the doctor cures King George by binding his knee and, "after a few moments, one of the actors, identity not known, falls to the ground and starts to groan." It is this non-combatant who has his tooth drawn. Bennell and Wege, H.C., XIX, 591–592.

Onians, pp. 229–237, deals with examples of birth from the tooth and beard-hairs; see above, n.30.

bury the hobby-horse dies and is revived by the laying-on of hands by Jan and Bet. Here it is apparently the heat that is the reviving agent.[18] This idea of heat is connected with the seasonal aspect of the ceremony and the rejuvenation of the earth with the warmth of the sun in spring.[r]

Perhaps the most interesting cure of all, however, takes place in a Sword Play from Bellerby, Yorkshire. It is here that there is a direct connection between the cure and fertility. After Bessie is executed the doctor goes through the comic business of lifting up her feet and saying, "Neck is broken," raising her head and saying, "Her things are out of joint and she is filling with wind causing her bowels to be in an uproar," and then presenting his pills to cure all ills, "time present, time gone and time to come." The directions then tell us that he "rubs Bessie's stomach and she arches her back." Not only do Bessie's movements indicate a birth process but the doctor's medicine is identified as "pennyroyal," a well-known abortant.[19]

The resurrection itself is invariably the most perfunctory part of the cure section of the play. After the doctor has administered his medicine, the victim simply revives. Occasionally he will complain of a backache or claim he has seen wonders, but never for more than four lines at the most. This appears odd, at first, since if one were looking for some parallel between the men's ceremonial and the ancient fertility ritual, he would expect some kind of major celebration to occur at the revival of the dead combatant. A celebration does indeed occur; but it has been unrecognized because of the usual division of the play and the loss, somewhere in its fragmentation, of the clearly connecting link. Nevertheless, if we look now at the *quête,* we can find the remains of the primitive celebration analogous to the *kōmos* of the Phallic Song.

The Quête

Three actions generally occur in the *quête* of the Hero-Combat: a procession of characters, an entertainment and a collection. When we look at the Wooing Ceremony, we will see still another, the invitation to the wedding feast.

[r] It also threads through the Doctor's speeches of the more normal cures, such as the one we have from Burghclere, Hampshire, which is not at all unusual. After applying one drop of his "golden foster drops" to the tongue and one to the head, the doctor claims it will "strike the heat to the whole of his body and raise him from the ground." Tiddy, p. 187.

The Procession of Characters. The characters of the *quête* procession
are generally figures who have not appeared before or, if they have, ones
who have had no direct connection with the combat. Most common
are Beelzebub with his club and dripping pan and Little Devil Doubt,
with a broom.[9] Beelzebub usually appears with a quatrain running something like

> In come I, Old Beelzebub
> Over my shoulder I carries my club,
> In my hand a dripping pan,
> Don't you think I'm a jolly old man?

Little Devil Doubt often follows right behind, introducing the collection with

> In come I, Little Devil Doubt
> If you don't give me money
> I'll sweep you all out

or

> Money I want and money I crave
> If you don't give me money
> I'll sweep you all to the grave.

It is these two characters more than any other whom scholars have
used with assurance to connect the men's ceremonial with the medieval
mysteries and moralities. And there is, clearly, some connection here.
Beelzebub and Little Devil Doubt appear to be direct descendants of
the Clowns and Vices of the moralities and even the devils of the mysteries, like Beelzebub and Satan's lesser assistants in plays such as those
of the York Mystery Cycle.[20]

But there is no evidence of any kind to prove that the Beelzebub and
Little Devil Doubt (or even St. George) of the men's ceremonial are
direct *lineal* descendants of the mystery or morality. Beelzebub, Devil

---

[9] One might try to find all sorts of philosophic and thematic clues in this
name but it is, finally, only a corruption of the contraction, "D'out," for "Do
out," which refers to the broom and the character's sweeping out of the old
year's ashes.

Doubt, Big Head, Johnny Jack, and all the similar comic figures of the *quête* are, rather, all different aspects of the same, interchangeable type of popular clown who captured the imagination and interest of the folk. There is little question that there was some exchange between the medieval drama and the men's ceremonial; but it is an example of infiltration and cross-influencing, the threads of which are so inextricable that it would be folly to try to untangle them. Tiddy recognizes this connection, but he, too, is careful not to commit himself to hypothesizing specific influences. The most he can do is allude to these characters as "links that unite the Mummers' Play, Mysteries, Moralities, interludes and literary drama." [R]

If the Beelzebub of the mysteries has a Christian figure at his base, the Beelzebub of the ceremonial, with his club and dripping pan, seems to have a more primitive antecedent.

Relevant to this, it should be noted that the figure of the "female," so essential to the action of the Wooing Ceremony, often appears in the *quête* of the Hero-Combat in the shape of characters like Mary Tinker, Mary (ain't been yit), Dame Dorothy, and Molly Masket. [21] There is good reason to believe that these two figures, the clownish Beelzebub and the "female," once did have a direct connection with the central action of the ceremony and lost their place in the Hero-Combat, as they did not in the Wooing Ceremony and some Sword Plays, when the combat began to take precedence over the direct fertility elements. Douglas Kennedy points this out when he calls the "female" and Beelzebub of the mummers' play "antiques" even though they are relegated to minor and apparently unrelated roles. He says:

> With European analogies to guide us, especially primitive phallic examples in Rumania and Macedonia, the Clubman and the reproducing female are essential to the fertility cult. It is the basic cult and not the names of the characters that distinguish the real Plough Play from the Mummers' Plays which depict only death and resurrection. [S]

[R] Tiddy, p. 112. "Make every possible allowance for the universality of the dramatic instinct and even so, it is still difficult—to me it is impossible—not to believe that the Morris fool, the Doctor's man, Beelzebub, the fool of the Mummers' Play, the clown of the Sword Play, the devils of the Moralities and the Interludes are all, by dint of their mischief or their black faces or their fooling, ultimately one and the same."

[S] Kennedy states this in a footnote to M. W. Barley, "Plough Plays in the

There is a dangerous tendency, particularly in the field of folklore and anthropology, to jump to phallic conclusions as soon as anything remotely cylindrical appears in ritual. Nevertheless, if we look at the Beelzebub of many of the Wooing Ceremonies and his behavior with the "female," and if we look at the fool of the Sword Play as well as the uncompromisingly explicit behavior of the analagous clubmen of the Rumanian Kalusari dancers (see Appendix G) and the characters of the mummers' plays of the southern Balkans, we can find support enough for this view that Beelzebub's club is directly descended from the phallus of the fertility ritual.ᵀ Kennedy takes this idea even further and brings in the dripping pan which Beelzebub invariably carries in his other hand as a female characteristic.²² This is a most interesting and perceptive insight. It not only throws light on the presence of Beelzebub in the Hero-Combat, but as we shall see, supports theories about the significance of the "lock of swords" in the Sword Play.

If we accept this idea of the Hero-Combat's Beelzebub as a remnant of a central fertility figure who has become displaced by the combat

---

East Midlands," *JEFDSS,* VII (December 1953), 90, n.47. Kennedy, however, uses the term "man-woman."

E. K. Chambers, *The Medieval Stage,* I (Oxford, 1903), 215–216 discusses all the *quête* characters as figures who had once had a direct bearing on the action but have now fragmented off and become dislocated, though persistently retained.

ᵀ A relationship can also be discerned here between the function of these club-bearing figures and the god, Priapus, son of Dionysus and Aphrodite. Priapus was generally regarded as the god of fruitfulness and was represented with an enormous phallus. Sometimes he was represented as an old man with a long beard, a large phallus, and fruit and bunches of grapes in his lap, bringing together the male and female characteristics of fecundity in one figure. Chaucer does precisely this in *The Parliament of Fowls,* when he describes a statue of Priapus which

> Withinne the temple in sovereyn place
> stonde,
> In swich aray as whan the asse hym
> shente
> With cri by nighte, and with hys sceptre in
> honde.
> Full besyly men gonne assaye and fonde
> Upon his hed to sette, of sondry hewe,
> Garlondes ful of freshe floures newe.

The Poetical Works of Chaucer, ed. F. N. Robinson (Cambridge, Mass., 1933), lines 254–259.

once the magic of the ceremony has faded, we have yet another link with the other two types of death and resurrection ceremony we are studying here. And we have yet more reason to assert that they find their source in a single ritual.

There is a wide variety of characters who appear in the *quête* besides Beelzebub and Little Devil Doubt. Many of them are familiar stock characters, like Johnny Jack (with my wife and family at my back), Tosspot, Big Head (and little wit) and a musician who goes under any number of names but whose major purpose is to accompany the entertainment that is part of the *quête*. Often a character like Jolly Jack, Tosspot or Big Head will turn out to be the musician himself.[u]

Two other significant *quête* types who often appear are the hobby-horse and caricatures of real figures.

At first glance the hobby-horse that appears in the men's ceremonial seems to be simply an occasional grafting from another ritual. However, as one moves more deeply into a study of the play, the number of appearances of animal disguise becomes astonishingly high. In Cheshire and Dorsetshire, the hobby-horse is almost a constant element and those plays from these areas in which he does not appear are atypical. Besides his actual appearance in the *quête,* we can also find traces of him in the cure sections of the plays in every county of England. Sometimes we encounter him as the "doctor's horse," like the one in Thenford, Northamptonshire, where a player carries the doctor on his back and supports his hands on a small stool as he moves along.[23] In other plays he does not appear at all, but is "left outside" while the doctor and John Finney perform an elaborate, comic, servant-master routine reminiscent of Plautine comedy.[v]

---

[u] In Waterstock, Oxfordshire, for instance, Jack Finney suddenly assumes the character of Bighead and introduces the entertainment with,

> In Comes I that ain't never been yit,
> With my great head and little wit.
> My father killed a great fat hog and this
> you may plainly see is the old bladder
> out of his old hundy gurdy dee.

He then proceeds to use it to accompany the Finishing Song. Tiddy, p. 208.

[v] Douglas Kennedy, "Observations of the Sword Dance," *JEFDS,* 2nd s., III (1930), 36–37, has worked out an ingenious thesis that Jack Finney, the doctor, and the hobby-horse were originally one and the same figure, the life-restorer, but split off as representational sense and comedy assumed more importance.

It is in Cheshire and Dorsetshire, however, that we can see most clearly the hobby-horse's direct connection with the fertility ritual. In Cheshire it is made out of a dead horse's head which has been boiled and then used as the base of the ceremonial horse. His driver often calls attention to the resurrection element in this with *quête* verses like the one we have from Comberbach:

> In comes Dick with all his men
> He's come to see you once again,
> He once was dead and now he's alive
> And what you can see of him but a poor old
>   horse's head and one leg;
>   and for his living he's obliged to beg.[w]

In the plays of Dorsetshire, the hobby-horse serves yet another purpose, one which we shall find important when we look at the analogies between the *kōmos* of the Phallic Song and the *quête*. This purpose is that of divination and prophecy. The horse has a long history of associations with ecstatic divination, not only in England, but all over the primitive Western world.[24] By the time we see it in plays like those in Evershot and Symondsbury, that prophetic quality has turned into an excuse for abuse and social satire. After Tommy the Pony has been resurrected in Symondsbury, Bet claims he is able to tell fortunes. She proves it by telling Tommy to go through the crowd of spectators and search out "the boy that pinches his mother's sugar," which Tommy does, and "the little girl who throws the bedclothes off in the morning whilst dreaming about her sweetheart." [25] Innocuous as these exposures are, one can see the remains here of the opening for a far more savage kind of invective and abuse.[x]

We see a similar kind of satire occurring in the appearance of the caricatures of real figures. Oliver Cromwell is frequently encountered as a *quêteur,* sometimes even the defeated combatant, particularly in Irish versions of the play. His words almost always contain some reference to

---

This action is supported by action like the kind we find in Brill, Buckinghamshire, in which the doctor actually enters on the back of John Finney and is finally thrown. Harmon, p. 190.

[w] H.C., I, 65. See Appendix H on the horse's head in the Cheshire Souling Play.

[x] The horse as prophet is also found in the Isle of Man Laare Van ritual.

his "copper nose." More recently, in Heptonstall, Yorkshire, the "female" introduced himself with

> In come I, a suffragette
> Over my shoulder I carry my clogs.[26]

When the figure of Twing Twang appears, he calls himself "the leader of the press gang," alluding to the late eighteenth and early nineteenth century system of impressment into the naval service.[Y]

The folk have found openings in other sections of the play for social satire, invective and abuse. In Hampshire, a lawyer is called in before the doctor to help clear the Valiant Soldier of his crime. The lawyer asks how much the Valiant Soldier has.

> VAL. SOL.: Two shillings in money
> One wife, one son;
> When that's set down the bill is done.

The lawyer asks ten guineas and a glass of grog, and continues,

> I am supposed to take your cap, boots and
> clothes, and if I had a lawyer's right, I
> should take your life as well.[27]

The words "(ad lib)" after the lawyer's speech here, confirm the idea that this is a section open to improvisatory abuse of the profession. Nevertheless, it is in the *quête* that we see the players taking the opportunity for social satire and personal abuse most clearly. This, I believe, is because it was one of the original purposes of the ritual.

[Y] We also have examples of more localized abuse and satire. When the Large-head-and-little-wit figure appears in the Edith Weston, Rutland, version, he refers to himself as Albert Hart. This can only be a specific local allusion. V. B. Crowther-Brynon, "Morris Dancers Play," *The Rutland Magazine,* II (1905), 108. H.C., XIX, 511.

Similarly, a figure called Jarve Elwood appears only in Kirton-in-Lindsay, Lincolnshire, with these words,

> In comes I, Old Jarve Elwood, as bold as a lion,
> A grand new shop and not much iron,
> A pair of bellows full of holes
> A rusty old stiddy and not many coals.

Ordish Collection (n.d.), H.C., IV, 3.

The Entertainment and Collection. What I have chosen to call the "Entertainment" section of the *quête* generally occurs in direct connection with the collection. It operates as a Finishing Song. The Askham Lincolnshire Jolly Boys play affords us an excellent, fully developed example of the most common form of the entertainment.[28] The *quête* begins with the kind of procession we have just been looking at. Bold Bonny calls in Mother Askett (On my arm I carry my basket) and Beelzebub, who says:

> I am old Beelzebub. Under my arm I
> carry my drum.
> In my hand I carry my can. I think
> myself a jolly man.[29]

Here is another example of one of the major *quêteurs* doubling as musician. After Beelzebub, the Finishing Song begins and it is here that we can see the collection inextricably bound up with the entertainment.

Enter Bessie Brownbags dancing about

All sing "The next that come in is old Bessie
   Brownbags.
  For the sake of her money she wears
   nowt but rags."
All dance Foll-di-dee, foll-di-dee, foll-di-
   diddle die dom day."
  Foll-di-dee, foll-di-dee, foll-di-
   diddle die dom day,
  Oh here we go round and round all in
   a row,
  The finest young fellows that ever you
   saw.
  Foll-di-dee, foll-di-dee, foll-di-
   diddle die dom day.
  Put your hands in your pockets and
   pull out your purse,
  And give us a trifle, you won't feel
   much worse.

All continue singing chorus at they dance out [30]

The entertainment can take many other forms unrelated to the collection. At its simplest it takes the form of Christmas carols which end the entire performance.[z]

The Quête and the Kōmos

In his study of the Phallic songs in *The Origin of Attic Comedy*, F. M. Cornford divides the scheme of the ancient ritual into three major sections: a procession to the place of sacrifice, the sacrifice itself, and the procession resumed with a *kōmos* song addressed to Phales. In its relation to Aristophanic comedy, Cornford sees the *kōmos* as a survival of the bridal procession and the Sacred Marriage and the ensuing feast as a survival of the Wedding Banquet.[AA]

If we look at only four of Cornford's major points, an interesting parallel emerges between the *kōmos* of the Phallic procession and the *quête* of the Hero-Combat. The first is the very processional nature of the *kōmos* itself; the next is the nature of the leader of the Phallic Song; the third is the structure of the song; and the fourth is in connection with the elements of invective and abuse.

In the Phallic Song, the procession is resumed with the *kōmos* after the sacrifice. Theodor Gaster elaborates on this in his Editor's Foreword to Cornford's work.

> A merry, rambunctious *kōmos* provides an appropriate finale for any comedy or farce, but in the case of the folk play it also serves a more specific purpose. Such plays are usually performed by an itinerant troupe that makes the rounds, like carol singers, from house to house. In such a setting, the final *kōmos* provides a means of rounding up the company

[z] In Lydiard, Wiltshire, the entertainment seems to function like the jigs of the Elizabethan playhouses. After a fairly conventional multiple combat and cure and a *quête* appearance of Beelzebub and Saucy Jack we are told, "Here St. George and Tinker quarrel and fight. Tinker sings." The oddity of this is that he sings a courting song, "Good morrow Moll and 'ow dost so," and St. George suddenly assumes the role of the "female." Then follow, one after the other, a Robin Hood song by Tinker, "He that courts a pretty girl," by St. George, and "Away to the greenwood tree," by Saucy Jack. Alfred Williams, "A Wiltshire Mummers' Play," *Wiltshire Gazette,* December 30, 1926, p. 3.

[AA] Cornford, pp. 64–66. This has been considerably modified by Theodor Gaster with the recognition that the *kōmos* upon which Aristophanes was structuring the final sections of his plays was really no more than the equivalent of a collegiate binge. See Gaster's Introduction to Cornford, p. xxiv.

at the end of the performance and of marshaling them in procession before they move on.[31]

This is precisely what we see happening in the *quête* of the men's ceremonial. We have already discussed the processional nature of the entire
performance and have seen how the play is structured to support this
element (see above pp. 14–17). We can see it even more clearly if, in
addition to the *quête* of the Hero-Combat, we look ahead for a moment
to the *quête* of the Wooing Ceremony.

In the Plumtree, Nottinghamshire, Plough Monday Play we have a
fairly standard version of the prologue and *quête*. Both are initiated by
Tommy, the Fool. At the beginning he enters alone, while the other
performers wait outside until he gets the master and mistress' "consent
they s'all all come in." [32] When they do come in, it is clearly in procession, for at the end of the action we are told that the clown goes out first
and as the others "go out in the same order they came in," they sing,

> Good master and good mistress
> You see our fool has gone;
> We take it in our business to follow him along.
> Goodnight and thank you very much.[33]

With the clown initiating it, therefore, we have exactly the marshaling
of the company for the procession which Gaster describes.

The initiation of the first as well as the final movement of the action
by the clown also allows us to look into the nature of the leader of the
procession. In the Wooing Ceremony, he is the Clown, or Fool. In the
Sword Play, it is the Captain or Fool who sings the Calling-on Song. It
is, however, in the "antique" Beelzebub of the Hero-Combat that we can
see our clearest association between the leader of the *quête* and the leader
of the Phallic Song. We have already seen the links between Beelzebub
and some ancient fertility figures. If we also note the fact that his face is
typically blackened, and then look at a description of the derivative performance of the Phallophoroi (phallus-bearers), the connection between
the men's ceremonial *quête* and its leader and the ancient Greek ritual and
its phallus bearer is astonishingly close.

> The Phallophoroi . . . wear no mask, but they put on a visor made of
> the flowers *serpyllum* and *paideros,* and above it they wear a thick wreath

of violets and ivy. Wrapt in thick cloaks, they enter [the theatre], some
by the side entrance, others by the central door (in the back scene),
marching in step and saying:

> This song to thy glory, Bacchus, we pour
> In simple rhythm with various tune;

> . . . .

Next they ran forward and satirised persons whom they had fixed on.
They performed standing still. The bearer of the phallus . . . was smeared
with soot.[BB]

Now by the time we have this description, the Phallic Song has evolved
into a relatively stationary performance in a theatre. Nevertheless, if
viewed in the light of analagous rituals, it is difficult to dismiss the idea
that the ancient figure of the leader of the Phallic Songs, the phallus-
bearer of the Phallophoroi and Beelzebub of the men's ceremonial did
at one time serve an identical purpose.

The choral form of the *kōmos* song is still another element which
immediately strikes us in the *quête* of the men's ceremonial. Cornford
compares it first to the work song or chanty where a leader sings the
verse and the other members respond with a chorus, either a repetitive
one, or one which develops the initial idea of the verse. The essential
feature, however, is the "alternation between a Chorus and a succession of
leaders." [34] Later he compares it directly with the songs "which accompany
the *quête* in the festal processions of many countries." [35] This is a feature
of any number of *quête* entertainments in the men's ceremonial. In the
Chithurst, Sussex, Tipteerer's play, for instance, we have "a dialogue between the Doctor and all the rest, who chant the answer in chorus:

DR. GOOD
  What time is it?
ALL
  Here's my watch and go right view it,
  Though there's no chain nor seals unto it.
DR. GOOD, TO THE NOBLE CAPTAIN
  Hip, Mr. Carpenter, I've got a little question to ask you.
  How far is it across the river?

[BB] Cornford, pp. 107–108. Note the similarity between this description and
that of the traditional men's ceremonial costume in Chapter Two, pp. 23–24.
Also, see above, footnote on p. 62 for a similar description of the god Priapus.

ALL

When you're in the middle you're halfway over—
Fol the riddle ido—
When you're in the middle you're halfway over—
Fol the ri the ray.

DR. GOOD

I know when you're in the middle you're halfway over, but that warn't
the question I asked ye.

*The Noble Captain turns away, and the Doctor prods him with his sword
and says*

Hip, Mr. Carpenter, I've got another little question to ask ye!
How deep is the river?

ALL

If you throw a stone in it, it will go to the bottom, *etc., and the whole
business is repeated, the next question being:*
How do you get across the river?

ALL

The ducks and geese they all swam over! *etc.*
and repeat asking
Whose house is that over yonder?

ALL

It is not yours but it is the owners, *etc.*
Next Question
How strong is the beer they sells?

ALL

If you drink too much it will make you tipsy!
etc.[36]

Since this is such a rudimentary and common form of folk song, too
much cannot be made of it as a direct link with the primitive Phallic
Song. It does, however, take on significance in establishing a relationship
between the *quête* and the *kōmos* song when we look at it along with
the other elements, particularly the "iambic" which follows the chorus
and which, in folk perambulations, "often takes the form of imprecations
upon the householder either of blessings if he give liberally or of the
reverse if he is stingy." [37] This parallels the form and content of the
Phallic Song, with its two elements of invective and invocation.

In the men's ceremonial we see the survival of this element in the
action of the hobby-horse, particularly when he becomes prophetic, and

in the abusive caricatures of contemporary and local figures. As it evolves, too, we see the invective shaded into the imprecations of blessings on the householder in Finishing Song verses like "God bless the master and mistress of this house."

Although the combat, death, and resurrection are the most accessible features in tracing the play back to its origins in the fertility ritual, the *quête* as an essential element in the form of the men's ceremonial has been too long overlooked as a key to the basic nature of the ceremony. It is a mistake, I believe, simply to dismiss it as an elaborate collection since it contains so many elements, although hidden and distorted by time, that support the concept of the men's ceremonial as a survival of an ancient fertility ritual. Indeed, as one looks at the men's ceremonial today, he finds that, although the death and resurrection have somehow managed to remain the obvious features which all the plays share, the entire performance has really become an excuse for an elaborate perambulatory *quête*. Tiddy describes the present state of the play as "a perfunctory piece of fooling that precedes the collection of money." [38] This is true, but if viewed in the light we have turned on the *quête*, there is less need for this embarrassed dismissal of the final section of the play as a gradual victory of the modern collection over the old ritual forms. In the retention of the processional and choral elements, as well as the collection, we really have as ancient a survival as the death and resurrection itself. It is, in fact, an even stronger survival; for this, far more than the ancient magical mime, has given the ceremony its present quality and its reason to survive. The modern men's ceremonial is, in short, its *quête*. It is as possible to trace its evolution back to the ancient fertility ritual through the action of its final moments as it is through its action of death and revival.

FOUR

THE SWORD PLAY

With the examination of the Sword Play, we move to Northeastern Great Britain, particularly Yorkshire, Durham, and Northumberland. Confined to a more specific geographical area as it is, the number of texts and accounts available to us is far less for this type of ceremony than for Hero-Combat versions. It is, in fact, small enough to allow us to choose three major examples to discuss in some detail, and only a handful of others to give us a sense of the common elements in all the plays. The three major documents are the texts for the Greatham Sword Dance Play, the Earsdon Play, and the Ampleforth Play.

The Greatham Text and the Sequence of Action

In his reproduction of the text of the Greatham Ceremony, Norman Peacock divides the action into four parts (see Appendix B for text). The first is the Calling On. This is followed by the First Dance. The third section is called "The Play" and the final one is the Second Dance.[1]

The Calling-On is begun by a character called Rantom Tom, with a speech similar to the prologue of the Hero-Combat.

> My master sent me here, some room for
>   to provide
> So therefore, gentle dears, stand back
>   on every side.[2]

Rantom Tom is one of two fools who appears in this play, both of whom wear old, patched clothes, and whose faces are blacked. He is also respon-

72

sible for most of the ribaldry that runs through the ceremony. Both
Rantom Tom and True Blue, the second clown, are equipped with "toy"
swords. Toward the end of his prologue song, Tom identifies his sword
as "Come strike if you dare." He then strikes at the air with it and follows
the action with

> So all you young lasses stand straight
>   and stand firm,
> Keep everything tight and close down,
> For if anything happens in forty weeks'
>   time,
> The blame will be laid on the clown.[3]

All these features—his introduction of the company, his blackened face,
his "toy" sword, the connection he makes for it with fertility and his
ribaldry—are particularly relevant to our discussion of the nature of the
phallus-bearer in the previous chapter.

Tom's prologue, an introductory call for room, takes only twenty-six
lines. The first ten are spoken, the rest sung. It is not until the King
takes over the action that the actual Calling-on verses begin.

But Tom does not even introduce the King. After his prologue, he
falls silent while Mr. Stout picks up a new tune and sings,

> Our King he will come in, dressed in
>   his granderie [grand array],
> He'll call his young men in by one by
>   two by three.[4]

The King then begins walking in a counter-clockwise circle and calls
in each of the dancers with two lines, naming and characterizing them
in some way. As they are called, they follow him in his circular movement
and respond with two more lines of self-introduction until all six dancers
are circling the dancing area counter-clockwise. This constitutes the true
Calling-on Song, and through it we can still discern the shape of the
familiar antiphonal song of the seasonal luck-bringing procession similar
to the choral song of the *kōmos*.

In turn, the King names Mr. Sparks ("lately come from France"),
Mr. Stout ("As good a swordsman he, as ever took sword in hand"),
Mr. Wild ("He has travelled a good few mile; But I'm afraid the worst

of all, these young maids he'll beguile"), the Squire's Son ("He'll lose his love because he is too young") and a Prince ("born of noble fame; He spent a large estate the wars for to maintain"). When they are all assembled, the two clowns introduce themselves:

> Nay, but I'm the last mesel', my name
>   is Rantom Tom,
> And the lasses you've got here I'll
>   kiss them every one.[5]

The clowns, therefore, are not included in the King's Calling-on Song. After they have joined the company, the others sing,

> We are six dancers bold, as bold as
>   you can see,
> We have come to dance this dance to
>   please the company.[6]

Again, the fact that they call themselves six dancers suggests that the clowns are not direct participants, but figures set apart from the community of dancers. At this point, too, as in the Hero-Combat, one of their functions is that of collection.[A]

One important aspect of the Calling-on Song of the Sword Ceremony which has never been dealt with satisfactorily is the emphasis it places on sexual prowess and courtship. This is another important link with primitive fertility themes as well as a direct link with the Wooing Version of the English men's ceremonial. When we look at the Wooing Ceremony in the next chapter we shall see how the Calling-on Song is transformed into the self-introductory verses of the wooers. In the Sword Ceremony itself we can see the emphasis gradually shifting from these fertility elements to themes of combat until, with verses like those of Papa Stour, all sense of courtship is gone and the Ceremony is interpreted entirely as a "war-dance" (see Appendix E).

Yet another prologue introduces the "Play" section of the Greatham

---

[A] We find this out later in the chorus when the six dancers sing:

> It's not for greedy gamble this ramble
>   we do take,
> But what you please to give our clowns
>   will freely take.

Ceremony. This time it is the second clown who calls for room, but with fascinating variations. His first four lines are the familiar *quête* words of the Hero-Combat,

> Here come I that never come yit,
> With my big head and my little wit:
> Although my head be big and my wit be small,
> I can act my part as well as you all.[7]

He calls for room, suddenly identifies himself as Bold Hector (after having already called himself True Blue in the Calling-on Song), and pursues a dialogue with the King which will culminate in his own execution. This dialogue begins with lines common to the dialogue between the Fool and the Recruiting Sergeant of the Wooing Ceremony,

> KING
> > I'm the King of the Conquerors
> > And here I do advance.
> CLOWN
> > And I'm the ragged clown
> > And I've come to see you dance.
> KING
> > Dance a dance! Hast thou come to
> > see a king dance?
> CLOWN
> > Lord ha' mercy, crack a bottle: if
> > thou was only 'anged in t' morn I'd
> > mak' a better King mesel'[8]

The clown continues to speak impudently until the King calls to the dancers to "try your rapiers on the villain." The Prince announces to the Clown, "There is bad news to come," and informs him he's to be tried for sheep-stealing. There is no real trial. The Clown simply says, "Worse news there couldn't be," and the King replies, "Yes, if we take thy head off."

It is here that the lock is formed about the Clown. Each dancer crosses the hilt of his sword loosely over the point of his neighbor's as they turn clockwise around the Clown. When the time comes, these loose positions will be tightened and the swords will lock in such a way that they can all be raised in a perfect hexagon by one man holding the hilt of one sword. The lock is never actually raised in Greatham, although it is a common occurrence in other ceremonies. It is used, in Greatham, as we shall see, only for the startling execution which is to follow. Before that, however, while the hilts and points are still crossed loosely and the dancers are circling around him, the Clown makes his will. He leaves his cow to one son, telling him to take good care of her, to which the entire company of dancers replies, "So I will, dad!" To his second son he leaves his lapp-board and shears, warning him to make good use of them; again the entire company answers, "So I will, dad!" He leaves his third son, Fiddler, his "backbone for fiddlesticks, small bones for fiddle strings," and finally turns to the King and says:

> And as for you, I'll leave thee the
> ringbone of my eye for a jack-whistle.
> So ladies and gentlemen, all, I bid you
> farewell.[9]

The dancers tighten the lock around the Clown's neck, then draw their swords abruptly. With the sharp, sudden sound of steel against steel and the single, swift withdrawal the Clown falls. The execution has been effected.

Now comes a rapid denial of responsibility, with two lines sung by each of the men involved. The King blames Mr. Sparks; Sparks blames Mr. Stout; Stout blames the Squire's Son; the Squire's Son denies his guilt and claims his eyes were shut. Before any resolution is reached, all the dancers decide to bury the corpse in the churchyard mould. The singing ends here, and the Prince says,

> Bury him! Bury him! How do you mean to
> bury him when all these people are
> standing around? If you mean to save life,
> send for a doctor out of hand.[10]

The King calls for the Doctor and the action moves into the familiar cure sequence we have already seen in the Hero-Combat, with the travel boast, fee haggling, and a most elaborate cure boast which contains familiar figures like

> Take these my pills to cure all ills—
>   the past, the present and to come.
> The gout, the itch, the sores, the stitch,
>   the money-grubs and the burley-stubs.[11]

and a number of figures which once again connect the Doctor's cure directly with fertility. He refers to his medicine as "white drops of life," offering them to any young woman in the company and then goes on to claim

> . . . when I was late in Asia, I gave two
>   spoonfuls to the great Megull, my
>   grandmother,
> Which caused her to have two boys and three
>   girls.
> She was then the age of ninety-nine, and
>   she swore if she lived nine hundred
>   years longer, she would never be with-
>   out two spoonfuls of this excellent
>   cordial of mine for a safe deliverance
>   on a cold and frosty morning.
> Two spoonfuls will cure the cuckle and take
>   away its horns.[12]

He then administers repeated doses to the Clown who finally rises and sings the conventional verses found in all three types of ceremony,

> Good morrow gentlemen, a-sleeping I have been;
> I have had such a sleep as the likes was never
>   seen;
> But now I am awake and alive unto this day,
> And now we'll have a dance, and the Doctor
>   must seek his pay.[13]

at which the second dance, the final section of the ceremony, begins.

The sequence of action that we find in the Greatham text, then, is prologue and creation of the dancing area; Calling-on Song; First Dance; second prologue, again clearing room for playing; the Clown's sauciness to the King which acts something like the challenge of the Hero-Combat in leading us to the execution; the formation of the lock and the making of the will; the execution; the unanimous denial of responsibility; call for the Doctor; cure and second dance.

Besides the nature of the Clown in Greatham, there are other features of the play which should strike us as familiar by now. One is the establishment of the father-son relationship in the Clown's making of the will and the dancer's responses. Another is the presence of Wooing Play fragments such as the early dialogue between the Clown and the King, as well as the appearance of the Squire's Son who characterizes himself with Wooing Ceremony verbal figures as an unlucky suitor. Finally, we have the complicated dance itself, treated as an entertainment during which the collection takes place.

Let us now look at two other major examples of Sword Ceremonies for common actions, and see what they suggest to us about the development of this type of ceremony.[B]

The Earsdon Dance: The Old Version and the Buophonia

From the action of Greatham, we can now move on to the Earsdon Sword Dance. The documentation of this play is of great importance. It gives us two versions of the ceremony, one called the "Old Version," and one designated as modern.[14] The fact that the more elaborate version, which includes the play and the execution, is called the "old version" and the one with nothing more than an introductory Calling-on Song is the modern, should support our idea of the comparative authenticity of the play of the Greatham Ceremony.

The old version of the Earsdon ceremony begins directly with the Captain's Calling-on Song of ten verses in which the dancers are characterized by their craft. The dancers are the Pitman, the Collier, the Tailor, the Ship's Cook and Big Walloping Tom. The last figure may well be a remnant of Rantom Tom, the Clown, since his characterizing verses deal

---

[B] The Bellerby, Yorkshire, play, whose cure we noted earlier, is quite close to that of the Greatham Play. It contains all the same actions as Greatham, but the sequence of their appearance is entirely different. This is not uncommon and it is for this reason that we must look for the common actions in our analysis of the sword play rather than the common structure as we did in the Hero-Combat.

The Bellerby play appears in Maud Karpeles, "Some Fragments of Sword Dance Plays," *JEFDS*, 2nd s., II (1928), 35–36. H.C., I, 260–261.

with wooing and courtship in exactly the manner of Greatham.[c] These Calling-on verses, however, do not lead into the dance, but into a death which emerges from action closer to that of the Hero-Combat than the Sword Play.

Before moving on to this, however, we must look at the final verse of the Calling-on Song which has some relevance to the problem of origins and primitive analogies. After the Captain has introduced all five dancers, he sings,

> Now I'm going to kill a bullock,
> Of that I'll make sure;
> We'll kill it in Earsdon town
> And divide it amongst the poor.[15]

This is a startling verse and one which is not recorded in any of the other versions of the Sword Ceremony that I have looked at.[D] No bullock is killed in the Earsdon play, although one dancer dies in combat and is resurrected and the Bessie is "hung" with the lock. What, then, is the relevance of a figure like this? Where does it originate?

Standing alone, it appears to have no relevance at all. If we look at it in connection with the repudiation sequence we have already seen in Greatham and as well in fragmentary form in Earsdon; and if we look

[c] Sharp, p. 85.

> The next that I'll call on,
> It is Big Walloping Tom;
> He's courted two fair women
> And durst not marry one.
>
> For if he married one,
> The other he would slight
> And the best thing he can do
> Is to treat them both alike.

[D] E. K. Chambers, *The English Folk Play* (Oxford, 1933), p. 150, connects the Ampleforth Clown's lines,

> I can stick a young heifer and never draw
>   blood
> And that I can do to a hair,

with the Earsdon verse. But the contexts of the two lines bear no relationship to each other. The Ampleforth Clown includes it as part of his nonsense speech telling about his own character. The Earsdon Captain points it up as an intended community action in his Calling-on Song.

at it in connection with form of the execution in the Sword Ceremony as a community action, this verbal figure helps to reinforce the idea of an analagous relationship between the ritual death and resurrection of the men's ceremonial and yet another primitive fertility action: the Buophonia, or ritual ox-murder.

Jane Ellen Harrison describes this ceremony in some detail in her chapter dealing with the nature of sacrament and sacrifice in the totemistic period of Greek religion.[16] In the Buophonia, an ox is murdered for a communal feast. Before the flesh can be eaten, however, the blame for the murder must be fixed. This shifts from participant to participant in exactly the manner of the Sword Ceremony repudiation sequence until the responsibility falls on the ax. Once the guilt of the ax is established, the ox is flayed, all the flayers taste the flesh and the flayed hide is then stuffed with hay and set up *just as it was when it was alive*. The participants then yoke a plough to it. In her analysis of the ceremony, Harrison says:

> the ox is brought to life again, not because they want to pretend that he has never died and so to escape the guilt of his murder (though later that element may have entered), but because his resurrection is the *mimetic representation* of the new life of the new year and this resurrection is meant to act magically.[17]

What we have, then, is the same death and resurrection we have been looking at and which we will see recur constantly throughout Europe. With the Buophonia, however, we have this action in the totemistic stage of a civilization's religious development.

There is here, too, a clear analogy between the resurrected stuffed ox and the hobby horse who is so often characterized as "once dead, now alive" and whose base is the boiled head of a real horse.

The sense of the communal feast is suggested in the final two lines of the Captain's verse. This, too, we shall see as a major element of the Wooing Ceremony in the Clown's invitation to his wedding feast.[E]

The Earsdon death occurs in the manner of the Hero-Combat. Immediately after the Captain's song, the first two dancers "feign a quarrel, fighting with their swords until one of them is wounded and falls to the ground. Whereupon there is a great commotion."[18]

[E] Although it cannot be brought in as valid supporting evidence, one wonders, too, whether the Clown's parcelling out of the parts of his body to his slayers in the will of the Greatham ceremony does not spring from some obscure sense of the communal, sacramental nature of the action.

The cure section is initiated by the Bessy, who cries "An actor he is dead . . ." and fears the company will suffer for it. In a fragment which is clearly the remains of the repudiation sequence we have already seen in Greatham, the third dancer disclaims responsibility for the death, the fourth dancer suggests they bury the victim and the fifth summons the doctor who arrives with his boast and cure.

Once the cure is effected, Bessy calls for the dance. Then the Bessy is "hung." Mr. Armstrong, the Captain of the Earsdon team in 1910, gave Cecil Sharp a description of the hanging of the Bessy:

> The Bessy . . . used to wear a hairy cap, and when the Nut was about to be tied, the dancers would sometimes call out, 'we'll hang the Betty'; whereupon, Bessy would step into the center of the ring and swords would be locked tightly around his throat while the dancers stepped.[19]

Apparently the Earsdon lock or nut was formed in a manner similar to that of Greatham, but it occurred outside the rather odd, atypical action of the death and resurrection, and there is no evidence from this description that a mock decapitation was effected with the lock. It would appear, at first, that what we have in Earsdon is the form of the execution retained without the basic mimetic action itself. But this is the kind of apparently obvious conclusion we must make only with the most extreme caution. When we discuss the nature of the shift of the ritual into myth in the final chapter, it will become evident that there is just as strong a possibility that what we have in Earsdon is the older *formal* action of the ceremony whose meaning has become lost or obscured, while in the clear mimetic execution of Greatham we have a much later explanation or rationalization of that earlier, formal movement.[F]

Bessy's line in this play, "An actor he is dead," is of particular interest to us, too, in illuminating a feature of the later changes in the play. E. C. Cawte has shown how this is an example of the movement from verbal corruption to corruption of sense which finally leads to a thorough distortion of the action itself.[20] In an account from 1857, we have a bizarre

---

[F] Indeed, in the case of Earsdon, particularly, it is difficult to accept the idea of execution in the hanging of the Bessie. Armstrong does not mention the swift drawing of the swords to break the Nut, which is the signal for the death of the victim in Greatham and Bellerby. This is because it would have been an impossibility. The Earsdon ceremony is a "rapper," or short sword dance in contrast to the long sword ceremonies of Greatham and Bellerby. As E. C. Cawte has noted, if the entire execution action were performed in the manner related by Sharp, the Bessie would have been killed in earnest. H.C., Index, Earsdon, Northumberland, sheet 1, note 1.

description of the death and resurrection as it occurs in a Durham Sword Ceremony. Before the dance concludes, we are told,

> grace and elegance have given place to disorder and at last all the actors are soon fighting. The Parish clergyman rushes in to prevent bloodshed and receives a deathblow. While on the ground, the actors walk round the body and sing as follows, 'Alas, our Parson's dead.' [21]

The obvious question that arises here is, "What on earth is the village parson doing taking such an active part in a ceremony which so clearly has its roots in primitive magic?" The answer lies in tracing the verbal corruptions the ceremony has undergone. The 1857 version is a description of the ceremony taken from a yet earlier source in which the lines quoted are, "Alas, our rector's dead." [22] The description of the clergyman's rushing into the fray seems to be pure invention to explain this line and in the explanation, the "rector" has turned into a parson. But the word "rector" itself, as suggested by the words of the Earsdon text, is yet another corruption. In an earlier manuscript, from 1815, contained in the British Museum, the words read, "Alas, our *actor's* dead." [23] So it is the verbal corruption of this figure, a corruption strange enough to have to be explained, that leads to the thoroughly distorted account we finally get. Mr. Cawte has given us a vivid object lesson on the dangers of trying to impose obvious, modern, rational "meanings" on a ceremony whose actions have their roots in a reality utterly alien to ours. In this case, it is the explanation of an apparently meaningless verbal figure. It can also happen in terms of basic actions and we must always be on our guard against accepting the obvious explanation merely because it is the simplest and most "reasonable." The simplest may be based on an explanation itself, an already rationalized version of an action whose real meaning has long since been obscured.

The Earsdon Dance: The Modern Version and Insight into Its Development

Returning to the Earsdon documents, we must look briefly at the modern version of the ceremony.[G] We find here that the only portion of the play

[G] The modern version goes back to at least before 1900. A note in H.C., Index, Earsdon, Northumberland, sheet 1, note 1, tells us that G. Osborne, a member of the Earsdon troupe interviewed by E. C. Cawte joined the team ca. 1900." He knew nothing of the play of the older version.

which remains is the Calling-on Song. These verses, too, have undergone a transformation. The Captain is the only singer now and the dancers, once identified by their trade, are now the sons of heroes. As the Captain identifies each dancer, he relates the historical exploits of the father. The son of "Brave Elliott" is the first to appear. In connection with him, the Captain sings of his father's defense of Gibraltar against the Spaniards in the battle of 1780. Following him is the Son of Lord Duncan and verses about the defeat of De Winter and the Dutch at Camperdown in 1797. The next verse introduces the Son of Lord Nelson and tells of the defeat of the French on the Nile (1798). The next deals with the Son of Wellington and his father's exploits at Waterloo and "tarryvarry" (Talavera). The last dancer in the chauvinistic assemblage is rather surprising. He is the son of "Buonoparte." His father's victories are left unsung.

The Bessie and the Clown still accompany the Earsdon dancers, but they have become peripheral appendages, merely stepping in time on the outskirts of the circle of the dance. They appear to serve no function, not even that of abuse or fooling. They are there, it seems, because the force of tradition demands that they accompany the dancers; but their purpose is entirely gone. This affords an excellent example of the gradual fading of even major characters until, like the *quête* figures of the Hero-Combat, the reason for their appearance is entirely obscured.[11]

In comparing the old and new versions of the Earsdon text, we can see one phase of the gradual change of the Sword Ceremony from mimetic ritual to artistic entertainment. By the time of the new version, the interest has clearly shifted from any trace of affective magic to intricacy of design in the dance itself. The words have been reduced to the simple, introductory Calling-on verses sung by one man; the dancers have been transformed into representations of the sons of real historical characters. Folk ritual has developed into folk performance.

The Ampleforth Play and the Problems of Bowdlerization

Because of the clear separation between the play and the Calling-on Song of the old and new versions of the Earsdon dance, the literary and ritual

---

[11] The Winlaton Sword Dance is the same as the modern Earsdon version. The peripheral, meaningless nature of the Clown and Bessie is even more evident in a film of the Winlaton troupe where we see the two figures performing one, simple monotonous step outside the circle throughout the dance.

nature of the ceremony is comparatively easy to deal with. This is not the case with the Ampleforth Play. Here the literary borrowings have been assimilated into the traditional mimetic action. The strands are more difficult to unravel.

The problem is further complicated by the evidence we have of bowdlerization on the part of Cecil Sharp. The Ampleforth Play was first published by Sharp in Volume III of his *Sword Dances of Northern England*. Prior to that, however, he had sent a copy of the text to Chambers, apparently taken from his Field Notebooks. Chambers reproduces that manuscript in *The English Folk Play*. The text that appears in Sharp's *Sword Dances* contains some telling differences. Chambers alludes to these differences briefly in his introduction of the Ampleforth text, characterizing Sharp's changes as "sophistications." [24] Upon investigation, however, Sharp's deletions emerge more clearly as concessions to a Victorian sense of decency. Chambers, for instance, includes this portion of the second wooing action in his account:

> KING. Sure I this woman's worse than mad!
> Judge, gentlemen, as well as me
> In taking such a snotty lad,
> And despising such a spark as me.
>
> *King straightens himself up.*
>
> QUEEN. Spread your affections civilly
> And I shall tell you what I think.
> In you the smal. . . .
>   [This was apparently incomprehensible
>   to Chambers]
> There's no mistake to choose and wink.
> CLOWN. Pox take her! There's nowt to please
>   her with.
> So saving thy debauchery!
> KING. I'll call thee liar to the teeth!
> I'll will at that accepted be. [sic]
> I'll make thee lies to the town estate.
> But if I in my duty fail,
> But come to me and I'll call it my fate.
> CLOWN. Perhaps thou's got some tenement,
> Some palace on some Irish shore;
> Perhaps thou lives by three ha'pence rent;

It's enough for thee to rent withal.

KING. Now I'm maintained by sailor's wives,
When their husbands are out all in protence,
While you poor eunuchs leads poor lives,
And I am swaggering by my rents.[25]

Except for some minor punctuation and tense changes, this is how it appears in Sharp's Notebooks.[26] These lines do not, however, appear in Sharp's published account of the Ampleforth text.[I]

The cure section, too, has apparently been tampered with.[J] This information leads us, naturally, to suspect that Ampleforth is neither an isolated nor an uncommon case.[K] It is fortunate that we have at least the

---

[I] E. C. Cawte, H.C., Index, Ampleforth, has noted, too, that in one case Sharp seems to have simply substituted his own lines. The Calling-on verse for the "sparkly lad" in the Field Notebooks reads as Chambers reproduces it:

> The next he is a spanking lad,
> His father is a squire;
> For Betsy their sweet chambermaid
> He got a great desire.
> He huddled her, he cuddled her,
> Until he made her yield;
> But when the truth they came to know,
> He was forced to quit the field.

In Sharp, we are given the more innocuous:

> The next he is a sparkly lad
> With his broad sword in his hand,
> He'll show you honest sword play
> As any in the land.
> So now I bid thee come they way
> All with thy valiant spear
> For thou canst act a gallant part
> As well as any here.

[J] Frank W. Dowson, "Notes on the Goathland Folk Play," *TYDS,* XXVIII (April 1926), 36–37, quite openly admits to bowdlerizing and alludes directly to Sharp's practice in Ampleforth. The doctor's cure attempts are most elaborate in both versions. Dowson justifies his own omission of explicit details in reporting on the Goathland ceremony by explaining that "the part would not now be tolerated, either for coarse words, or for the actions. The late Mr. C. Sharp expunged this part, too, I believe, for his version of the Ampleforth play."

[K] Further evidence confirming our suspicion of the undocumented prevalence of coarseness and ribaldry comes from Bucknall, Lincolnshire. Mabel Peacock, MS., Ordish Collection, 1901, tells us that the Plough Play was "supplied by one of the actors to the Rev. J. Conway Walter, Langton Rectory, who says in reference

scant information about this kind of bowdlerization that we do, for it supplies another important link between the men's ceremonial and the European primitive analogies. We see this kind of coarse, obscene behavior as an integral and significant element in the Rumanian Kalusari play, the mummers' plays of the Balkans and we are told of it in the *kōmos*. It would indeed be helpful if our information about the form this behavior takes in England were more explicit, but after examining the kind of information we do have about ribaldry and its bowdlerization it is fair to assume that it is common enough to be pertinent to our investigation.

We can be certain, at any rate, that obscenity is an element in the Ampleforth Play and as we look at the action of the play we must keep it in mind. This situation is yet another reminder of how fragmentary our knowledge of the men's ceremonial will be if we rely on the printed text as anything more than a sketchy guide to the action.

The Ampleforth Play and Literary Influences

Let us now look at the Ampleforth Play and see what it does tell us. It is by far the most elaborate textual record we have examined so far, with five divisions, each division comprising a complete action in itself. The first two are complete and separate wooing actions; the third contains an elaborate version of the abusive dialogue between the King and the Clown; two Calling-on Songs, the dance and the execution form the fourth part; and the repudiation and elaborate cure sequence complete the fifth.

The action begins with a call for room, not by the Clown as in Greatham, but by the King himself. It is he, as well, rather than the Clown who tells of his wooings and asks help of the Clown. The Clown, taking the King in hand, introduces him to the Queen as his son, Ben. In the sequence that follows, the first three speeches are sung; the remainder is

---

to a version of the drama represented in his kitchen at Woodhall Spa about the year 1889, that he and Mrs. Walter withdrew, being disgusted with parts of it. Any Rabelaisian details are, I think, usually dropped out when cultivated people form the audience."

Alex Helm, H.C., VI, 95, notes, also the disparity between the two undated versions of the Harptree, Somerset, Hero-Combat in the Vaughan Williams Library Collection and the published version of 1927; see also F. B. Kettlewell, *Trinkum-Trinkums* (Taunton, 1927), pp. 58–60.

spoken. It is this wooing action, from the time of the Queen's entrance to the end of the First Part, which gives us our most direct evidence of literary influence. Whether it was simply assimilated by exposure to traveling companies or imposed by a single hand, we cannot tell. But there is no doubt that this section is a corruption of the Prue-Ben wooing scene of *Love for Love*.[27] The Congreve lines have been transformed into crude couplets and the woman's name has been changed to Susannah, but the whole shape of the Congreve scene has been retained. The Clown introduces the King as Ben, his son, home from the seas; the King inquires after his brothers, Dick and Val, and the Clown answers:

> Did not I write last summer
> That pale death has closed his sides? [28]

When left alone, the woman rejects the sailor for his crudeness. He pursues, but finally rejects her. This ends the first part of the performance.

Although no direct source has been found for it, the second part may well come from the professional stage, too. Many of the speeches in the first part would be utterly incomprehensible without knowledge of the original from which they were taken. The similar incomprehensibility of certain allusions in the second part, as well as the easy assumption of new characters by the same three players in Part Two, the consistency of a new, more ribald tone, and the sense of a corrupted form of witty aphorism with which the King and the Clown end this section, all point to a possible origin in the Restoration theater.[L]

Oddly enough, this part begins with a familiar traditional speech. The Clown enters with the "great head and little wit" *quête* lines and announces he has

> six fine lads
> 'll please you all.

[L] Chambers, p. 149, ascribes the source of this section to "a sentimental drama" which he calls *The Fool's Wooing,* also supposedly the source of the Plough Play. The action of this section, however, bears no resemblance to the wooing actions of the third type of ceremony, as we shall see in the next chapter. Rather than a series of rejections leading up to the final triumph of the Fool as we find it in the Wooing Ceremony, we have a woman stringing two men along without making any decision at all, the men confronting each other in their rivalry and, finally, making specific literary comment on the attitudes of women. The form of the Ampleforth action, therefore, as well as its language, bears no resemblance to the action of the Wooing Ceremony.

He follows with the Hero-Combat figure,

> My head's made of iron,
> My heart's made of steel,
> My hands and feet of knuckle-bone,
> I challenge thee out to feel.[29]

The King enters and we are told that the two players "rattle their swords together." This may represent some corrupt form of combat, particularly following the "iron head-steel heart" figure, but it is impossible to be sure from the scanty information of the text. This "sword rattling," at any rate, is followed by a verbal figure we have already seen to follow the abusive dialogue of the King and the Clown in the Earsdon play.

> How long will this unthinking fool
> Disturb us of our private see [privacy]? [30]

But instead of calling on the company of dancers to take the Clown away, the King calls for Fair Rose to "banish him from our company." The Queen enters as Fair Rose and, with the dialogue which Sharp expunged from his record in *The Sword Dances,* the King and the Clown proceed to woo her. The Queen leaves the two men unresolved as to whom she will finally choose. She exits and we are given two aphoristic observations by the King and the Clown.

> KING. Thou are a fool, O then say I,
>   My reasons are expounded clear.
>   For women may riddle but none can tell
>   By plain subtraction what they mean.
> CLOWN. Still greater fool than half than I!
>   If thou would know the certainty
>   Of what a woman says,
>   Is meant quite contrary way.[31]

Part Three consists solely of a comic dialogue between the King and the Clown which begins precisely as the similar dialogue in Greatham. The Clown claims he has come to see the King dance and accuses the King of stealing swine. This leads to some knockabout play in which the King tells the Clown, "thee must either sing a song or off goes your head," and proceeds to abuse him with his sword. The rest of the scene contains what is apparently supposed to be comedy; but with only the recorded words, it approaches incomprehensibility. The Clown sings a distorted version of two popular eighteenth century ballads, "How can I be merry and wise?" and "O love it is a killing thing." The King corrects him on both songs. After the King sings the second song correctly, they both exit.

This is odd, for at the beginning of the fourth part, the King and the Clown return immediately and, except for a new self-introduction by the King, seem to pick up the action that begins Part Four exactly where it stopped in Part Three. This corresponds to the action that followed the abusive dialogue in Greatham. It is here that the King calls the other dancers to remove the Clown. The dancers rattle their swords, but remain out of sight behind the door and, rather than calling them out at this point, the King joins them. This allows the Clown to deliver a long speech in which he introduces himself, supplies us with nonsense figures about his ancestry and his own abilities and proceeds to introduce the Calling-on Song which he, himself, will sing. This speech, too, corresponds to the prologue speech of Greatham. In this case, however, the King does not take over for the Calling-on Song. The Clown continues speaking as he calls in the King.

> The first that comes on is King Henry
>   by name.
> He's a King and a Conqueror too;
> And with his broad sword he will make
>   them to fall;
> But I fear he will fight me enoo.
> *King and Clown rattle swords together.*[32]

He then introduces the five other dancers, characterizing each with four lines of verse. They are Progallus, the King's General; a Gentleman from Cork, who is "witty and pretty in every degree" and will "sport" among the girls; Hickman, his rival; Jerry, characterized as "a passionate friend" who "follows his master, indeed," and, finally, a character with a description odd enough to warrant direct quotation:

> There's little Diana I'd like to forget
> Whose beauty shines much like our own;
> But if ever we do get our heads to the pot,
> We'll drink till it strikes fourteen at noon.[33]

We might interpret this as an atypical instance of the appearance of the "female" as one of the dancing company, but this is only the first of two sets of Calling-on verses and there is nothing in the second set to indicate that any of the dancers is a "female."

Another peculiarity of this set of verses is the relationship it seems to imply between the dancers. We have already seen Calling-on Songs that characterize the dancers as the seven champions and the sons of heroes, but nowhere do we get the sense of the kind of relationship we have in the first set of verses from Ampleforth. This relationship appears to be the basis for yet another wooing action with Hickman and the Gentleman from Cork as rivals and Jerry as Hickman's companion. This, again, sounds suspiciously like the kind of romantic contest we find so frequently in Restoration theater, complete with the "passionate friend" who "follows his master, indeed." If there were some specific model for these characters in Restoration literature, it would not be surprising to discover that the object of this rivalry was named Diana. At any rate there is evidence again of a conscious literary hand of some kind in this set of verses.

The final peculiarity about this set of Calling-on verses is that it leads nowhere. No dance is indicated. After all the dancers have been called, the only directions given are for the exit of the troupe.

As soon as they are gone, the Clown begins to introduce the second Calling-on Song. This time he refers to his men as heroes of Waterloo and commends them to the girls who are watching. When he enumerates them individually, he refers primarily to their youth and sexual abilities. There is no emphasis put on their heroism. The first dancer is called simply, "a handsome young man"; the next is a "bashful youth"; the third is the "spanking lad" whose verses Sharp bowdlerized; the fourth is "a rakish youth." All of these are characterized specifically by their sexual reputations. The "bashful youth," for instance, "drives a roaring trade" amongst the pretty wenches:

> And when he meets a bonny lass
> His valour is displayed.[34]

and the verse for the "rakish youth" runs:

> The next he is a rakish youth;
> I've heard his mother say
> She would give him good advice
> Before he went away.

> He was never to kiss a black lass
> When he could kiss a white,
> And when he met a bonny lass
> To stay with her all night.[35]

After all six men have entered, the Clown concludes

> So lasses prepare your lips,
> Else before your eyes
> These six lusty lads
> Will roll you in their arms.[36]

He calls for music and the dance is performed.

The execution occurs at the conclusion of the dance. According to Sharp's version, the victim is an outsider, in ordinary dress, who enters the ring and has the lock placed over his head. After his death, all the dancers leave the playing area to the Clown and the corpse.

After the opening sequence of Part V, the shape of the play becomes familiar. The first sequence is a short comic action leading up to the repudiation verses.

> *The Clown walks about and tumbles over the corpse.*
> CLOWN. It's rough ground.
> *Clown turns round and tumbles over again.*
> *King enters.*
> KING. Hello! Hello! What's the matter here?
> CLOWN. A man dead!
> KING. I fear you have killed him.
> CLOWN. No! He has nearly killed me! [37]

The King then introduces the repudiation sequence explicitly. He stamps his feet and calls out, "Come all you villians [sic] and clear yourselves!" All the other dancers participate in the shifting of blame until the Sixth Dancer accuses the King. This leads to a fight between the King and Number Six who "rattle their swords together" once again. In this elaborate version, the King finally takes the blame for slaying the "poor old man" and it is then that the Clown establishes the father-son relationship. "How can he be an old man," he asks. "Young man like me his father." [38] He decides they should bury the corpse, but first they must sing a Psalm over the body and read his will. The Psalm turns out to be a nonsense verse, repeated dutifully by the other mourners. The will runs simply:

> God in heaven take his soul!
> Churchyard take his bones!
> And that man, that holds my sword,
> Take his wife and bairns!
> *Clown hands his sword to another man.*[39]

After the reading the will, the King decides they cannot bury the corpse "when people all around us stand." They will have to call for a doctor to bring him to life again.

The doctor enters with pills that "cure the young, the old, the hot, the cold, the living and the dead," and the familiar fee haggling ensues between the Doctor and the King. The cure, itself, is an elaborate and inventive one. It begins with the administration of the pills. The King and the Clown question the wisdom of giving a physic to a dead man, but the Doctor assures them, "I can raise a stomach in the morning, make his victuals fly down his throat like a wheelbarrow, and rattle in his throat like a pair of chests of drawers."[40] This leads into a long boast which includes treatments such as "husband trimming," cure of the "big-bellied mare, the old fools, the gaol and the pepper vixit cracks," and the usual itch, stitch, stone, bone, pulse and gout.[M] After the boast the King calls attention to the fact that the corpse is still dead. The Doctor decides he must bleed him.

> *Doctor gives the King the dead man's arm to hold up and then runs at him with his sword. The King falls and knocks his knee cap off, which the Doctor then puts right. The Doctor then bleeds the dead man.*[N]

After this action the travel boast resumes with traditional nonsense figures found in the medieval *Land of Cockayne.*

> I've travelled all the way from Itti Titti where there's neither town nor city, wooden chimes, leather bells, black pudding for the bell rope, little pigs running up and down street, knives and forks stuck in their backsides crying 'God save the King.'[O]

[M] This section, too, is expunged in Sharp's published version.

[N] Chambers, p. 148. See also above, note on p. 58.

[O] *Ibid.,* p. 148. The medieval *Land of Cockayne* has been cited as a source or analogue for this figure by many commentators on the play. The fullest accounts are given by Tiddy, p. 116, and Chambers, p. 49.

The dead man has still not revived. This time, in a manner reminiscent of the Jack Finney sections of the Hero-Combat, the Clown decides he will try the cure. He "takes his sword and pulls it down the man's middle." This succeeds and the dead man jumps up, delivering the last speech of the play which ends with the promise of final entertainment and collection.

A close study of the Ampleforth Play in terms of its literary accretions and analogies with the more traditional plays yields some fascinating insights to the structure of the ceremony as a whole. Those elements which appear to have literary sources are the wooing fragments of Parts One and Two and the first Calling-on Song of Part Three. If we extract these elements, we find a sequence which contains nothing less than all the actions we have already seen in our studies of the play sections of Greatham and the "Old Version" of Earsdon. Beginning with the King's introduction in terms of his own wooing abilities in Part I, we can move to the Clown's introduction of himself in the traditional Big-head-little-wit speech of Part Two, then to the abusive dialogue between the King and the Clown which would lead to the second Calling-on Song. The rest of the ceremony carries elaborations of all the familiar Sword Play actions including the dance, the execution, the repudiation verses, the reading of the will, the decision to bury the victim, the call for the Doctor and the cure.

This, I believe, is one of the most valuable, and, I think, misunderstood contributions of Chambers' study of the play. In finding literary sources like *Love for Love,* his clarification of where certain peculiar fragments originate is not half so important as his clarification of where they do *not* originate. He helps us separate the traditional from the literary. The Ampleforth Play can be seen in the direct flow of the traditional ceremony once this separation is made.

The Common Action: The Linked Dance

It is impossible to define the structure of the Sword Ceremony as clearly as we did the Hero-Combat. As we look at the different versions of the play we see common actions recurring often enough to be taken as traditional, but the pattern of their appearance seems arbitrary. Nevertheless, we can extract those common actions from the three versions we have examined in detail and see what information they give us about the

men's ceremonial as a whole and the relationship of the Sword Ceremony to the other types of play. Those elements peculiar to the Sword
Ceremony, then, which should command our attention are the linked
dance, the lock, and the Calling-on Song. We have already examined
the significance of the repudiation verses and the community execution
and their analagous connection with the ancient Buophonia.

Certainly the most important element is the dance itself, and, strangely
enough, this is one of the most misunderstood and distorted actions in
all the men's ceremonial. The easy assumption that the dance is pyrrhic
in origin springs most clearly and logically from the concept of the links
as swords. They are certainly considered swords in the versions we have
today, even by the dancers themselves. But there is evidence that this is
a fairly late development, a logical one, but one that may have done a
great deal to distort the true nature of the ceremony.

If we look at the figures at the dance without any preconceptions
about their nature or purpose, we find that even in its most complicated
form, the "swords" have only three functions.

First, and most important, they serve as links in the formation of the
dancing circle. They are always held hilt and point, which would be an
odd and dangerous position if they were real swords.[P] This hilt and point
linkage holds the company together while they form the circle and
through every other figure of the dance, no matter new convoluted.

Second, they are used in the formation of the lock. It is only here, and
briefly in their occasional rhythmic clashing that they cease to serve as
links. Now the assumption has always been that since the execution is
performed by the lock, the instruments forming the lock must be swords.
It is just as possible, however, that if the lock is the executing agent, the
links have been transformed into swords to explain the action more ra-
tionally. As we shall see, however, the lock is often used in a context
with no connotation of execution at all.

The third use is one of rhythm. This is when the swords are clashed.
This has been taken as a pyrrhic gesture, but there is no substantial reason for this assumption, since the links are invariably clashed in rhythm
and only as a part of an introductory or concluding movement or as a
transitional movement between linked figures.

[P] Even though the links are, indeed, considered representations of swords by
the dancers in present-day ceremonies, their use as hilt and point links has been
retained. This inconsistency is another clue to the later development of simple
links to swords.

Despite the brief, rhythmic clashing and the making of the lock, then, the major function of the "sword" is simply as a link between the dancers who use it to form the enclosed dancing circle, that figure which plays such an essential role in the magical nature of any ceremony.[Q]

Before we discuss the implications of this concept of the dance as non-pyrrhic and the Swords as originally nothing more than links, it would be valuable to look at the information we have concerning the lock.

The Common Action: The Lock

Our earliest description of the sword dance ceremony goes back to 1555. It is Olaus Magnus' account of a sword ceremony in the *Historia de gentibus septentrionalibus*.[41] In this description, the lock, which is called "the Rose" is formed, broken, formed again and passed over the head of each of the six dancers. There is no execution action of any sort. This is also true of a number of other sword ceremonies in Great Britain. The formation of the lock itself is a key figure in practically every dance, while the execution with the lock is confined primarily to ceremonies with dramas attached.[R] In Winlaton and Lingdale, for instance, the lock is displayed, the two clowns appear, but no execution occurs. This consistent appearance of the lock and only sporadic use of it for decapitation has led some scholars of the Sword Ceremony to believe that the concept of the lock as the instrument of execution is a fairly late develop-

[Q] Alex Helm, unpublished MS. of lectures delivered at Keele University Folk Studies Conference, Summer, 1966, deals with this problem most fully. "I believe that the title 'Sword Dance' is nothing more than a convenient label," he says, "which became used in an effort to describe the implements the dancers held between them; the fact that these implements are nothing like swords is conveniently overlooked. There is some evidence for thinking that the so-called 'swords' have some connections with trade tools used in the everyday work of the performers themselves." Helm goes on to cite the Flamborough "sword" which is almost identical with the fisherman's weaving tools and the double ended rapper which is similar to the primitive scraping tool.

See also, Joseph Needham, "The Geographical Distribution," *JEFDSS*, I (1936), 1–45; Violet Alford and Rodney Gallop, *The Traditional Dance* (London, 1955), *passim.*; Violet Alford, *Sword Dance and Drama* (London, 1960), *passim.*

[R] Besides the versions discussed, the lock is used for decapitation in Gainford, Durham: Miss Alice Eddlestone, MS., Ordish Collection, 1893; Escrick, Yorkshire: Sharp, III, 31; Grenoside, Yorkshire: Sharp, I, 58; Kirkby Malzeard, Yorkshire: Sharp, I, 53; Ripon, Yorkshire: H.C., I, 198–202; Sowerby, Yorkshire: Karpeles, "Some Fragments," 43–46.

ment and that its primitive significance has to do more with magical restoration than death. In one figure, in places like Ampleforth and Haxby, the lock is passed around the circle over the heads of the dancers as it is in the Olaus Magnus account. Douglas Kennedy has seen in this the mimetic rolling of the sun across the heavens.[42]

Alex Helm takes this one step further and puts forth a theory that originally the lock had a stronger connection with the restoration of the victim than with his execution. Helm sees it operating as a "female principle." In discussing the decapitation by the lock, he says:

> Although the significance of the Lock appears well-known to the performers, this again, may be a rationalization. Alternatively, if the Lock could be looked upon as basically a means of restoring life rather than taking it, it probably makes better sense, particularly if it is taken as a symbol of the female principle placed over the head of a male performer to complete the union.[43]

He then goes on to discuss the Germanic sword dances in which the lock is used for raising characters in one way or another rather than cutting them down.

None of these theories is mutually exclusive. Each, in fact, may simply represent a different stage in the gradual fragmentation of the ceremony. If, for instance, we take Helm's concept as the most primitive, we can see in this the most basic form of magic using the most basic magic symbol, the circle. This later turns into the more representational kind of mimesis in the ritual imitation of the movement of the sun across the heavens. This only helps reinforce our concept of the ceremony as a seasonal ritual with the sun restoring the life of the dead year in spring. Finally, with the development of the links that form the lock into swords as the ceremony becomes more and more "explained", we get the representation of the execution as we have it today.

The important fact that must be noted here, however, is that even in the modern versions of the Sword Ceremony, the lock is not used exclusively for decapitation. It need not necessarily, then, have been originally made of swords at all but could have been formed with any kind of links whether they were artisan's tools, sticks or flexible wands.[s]

---

[s] We have evidence of sticks and flexible wands being used for figures in the sword dance both in England and in analagous ceremonies in Europe. See Violet Alford and Rodney Gallop, "Correspondence," *JEFDSS,* III (December 1937), 150–151, for examples from the Isle of Man and the Iberian peninsula.

This brings us back to our original investigation of the nature of the dance itself and its development to the present.

The Development of the Dance

If we view the sword dance as non-pyrrhic and the swords as nothing more than links, a relationship emerges between the Sword Ceremonies we have been discussing and the other two types of men's ceremonial far stronger than the common presence of the death and resurrection. In its most basic form it can be considered as a linked circular dance. In its use of the linked sticks, the formation of the magic lock, and the Calling-on Song which springs from the familiar antiphonal chorus of the seasonal luck-bringing perambulation, as well as the very basic death and resurrection actions, we can place the Sword Ceremony in the direct flow of the fertility ritual celebrating the death of winter and the rebirth of the spring.

With this ritual as the ceremony's origin, we can follow it as it splits off into two fairly distinct lines of development. On the one hand we have the growth of a representational performance springing from the need to make the ritual comprehensible. It is here that the links for enclosing the inevitable circle are explained as swords. With that explanation, the shape of the entire ceremony takes on the structure as we know it today with the lock as the executing agent and the dancers characterized as heroic combatants. At this point the way is paved for the elaborate literary accretions we have seen in versions like Ampleforth.

The other line of development moves in the opposite direction, away from any kind of representation. The emphasis here is on the artistic nature of the performance in terms of spectacle, complex figures and virtuosity. We see this first in the sword dances which have lost all their mimetic action, such as the Winlaton and Lingdale dances. But that is only the first step.

As the ceremony incorporates more and more complex figures and loses its ritual meaning, it finally achieves the spectacular effects of the morris dance. In this form the links have turned into handkerchiefs in one case, and there are some Morris sides which still work with sticks.[T]

[T] Sharp first put forward this theory of the relationship between the sword and morris dance in *Sword Dances*, I, 11.

Since Sharp there have been a number of studies supporting the theory of a common origin for the sword dance and morris. Helm, in his lectures, presents

Even in its most elaborate form, the morris still contains traces of that basic element of affective magic so important to our study of the evolution of the ceremonial. It lies in the seasonal appearance of the dancers, the wearing of the great, rosetted hats and, above all, in the attitudes of the dancers themselves. In an interview with one of the finest morris men in England today, I questioned him about the elements of magic involved in the morris. His answer was as revealing as is was thoroughly unconscious of its own implications. "Don't go looking for that magic nonsense in the morris," he said. "It's not like that at all. We only do it for a bit of luck."

With the available texts and present-day performances as our guides, then, we have tried to trace the Sword Ceremony through its changes back to an earlier period when its form was allied much more clearly to the other two types as a death and resurrection ceremony in Great Britain. We have seen the rationalization of the links which are used to enclose the dancing circle into swords and with them the development of the magical lock into the instrument of execution. With the repudiation verses and the communal slaying of the victim we have been able to discover an analogy between the action of the Sword Ceremony and the totemistic ritual of the Buophonia. All these elements point back to the seasonal death and resurrection ceremony similar to the one from which the Hero-Combat must have sprung.

Now let us look at the Wooing Ceremony, the type of the men's ceremonial that has probably retained its ancient form more clearly than either of the other two types.

---

another convincing argument for a common source by tracing the costumes of the two forms. The analogies between the Sword Ceremony costume and those not only of the morris but of the Hero-Combat, Wooing Ceremony, and Balkan mummers are extraordinary.

See also, Rodney Gallop, "The Origins of the Morris Dance," *JEFDSS*, II (1935), 35–41, and Joseph Needham, "The Geographical Distribution," *passim*.

FIVE

THE WOOING CEREMONY

In our investigation of the Hero-Combat form of the men's ceremonial, we saw a number of unassimilated figures hovering on the out-skirts of the central action. Although they had no function in the combat itself, they attached themselves to the action in an apparently arbitrary manner as *quête* figures. Among these were the "female," assuming forms like Besom Bet, Molly Tinker, and Bessie Brownbags, and one or more fools like Bighead, Jack Finney, Beelzebub, and Little Devil Doubt. In the Sword Ceremony these figures began to operate in more clearly defined areas. The clowns of Greatham began to play a direct role in the central action either as victims or leaders of the choral songs. In some cases, however, they still remained on the periphery of the action. They served no integral purpose but refused to disappear. This tenacity suggested ceremonial functions for these characters which, although now lost, must have been of central importance at some time in the ritual's history. This function can be found in what most scholars of the play consider its oldest form, the Wooing Ceremony.[1]

The "female" and the Fool play key roles in the Wooing Ceremony. They actually serve to define the shape of the action. Interestingly enough, when this occurs, the apparently extraneous *quête* sequences, and the figures which comprise them, disappear. We are left with an action which involves every figure of the troupe, an action that is far more unified than anything we have looked at so far.

The Wooing Ceremony is confined to four East-Midland counties—Lincolnshire, Leicestershire, Nottinghamshire, and Rutland. It is astonishingly consistent in form wherever it appears, even when it is wedded to some form of the Hero-Combat. In this chapter, therefore, I propose to look at only one complete example of the type and trace its pure line of action. With this sense of the action we can then look at the development of the Wooing Ceremony in terms of its early form, literary accretions and gradual shifts in emphasis.

The Bassingham Play

We have a rather complete account of a play in Bassingham, Lincolnshire, 1823.[A] This play begins with the already familiar Prologue. The Fool enters alone and announces that he has brought the troupe which is awaiting permission to enter.[B] The troupe then sings the choral song,

> Good Master and good Mistress,
> As you sit by the fire,
> Remember us poor ploughlads,
> That run through Mud and Mire.
>
> The mire it is deep,
> And we travel far and near.
> We will thank you for a Christmas Box
> And a mug of your strong Beer.[2]

Now the wooing action itself begins. The Eldest Son, the Farming Man, and the Lawyer woo the Lady in turn. She rejects them all. Before the action can be completed, however, a second "female" appears. This is Old Dame Jane. She enters, carrying a doll, and searches for the Fool. When she finds him, she says,

> Long time have I sought you,
> But now I have found you.
> Sarrah, come take your Bastard.[3]

The Fool, however, will have none of it. He claims that the Baby looks nothing like him, that he is a "Valiant Hero, lately come from Sea,"

[A] Baskerville, pp. 241–245, prints two versions of the Bassingham Play. The first is called the "Men's Play," and the other, the "Children's." That account described here is mainly that of the Children's, which is the more complete of the two. Reproduced in Appendix C.

[B] There are no line tags for the Fool, although the speaker of the Prologue says, "I will act the Fool to please you all." Actual tags do not appear until the entrance of St. George.

boasts of the number of men he has slain and threatens to add Jane to the number if she doesn't leave him alone.[c]

The wooing action resumes now, with the entrance of the Old Man. He claims he has set his heart on the Lady, but she rejects him, too, asking, "Do you think I'd marry such a Drone?" She claims she is looking for a man of high degree.

The wooing action is discontinued yet again, this time with the introduction of the combat in the form of the sudden entrance of St. George, who delivers the common history boast and challenges the Fool. They fight. The Fool falls and Dame Jane calls for a doctor, "my husband to cure." The Doctor arrives. There is a typical cure dialogue between Dame Jane and the Doctor, and the Fool is resurrected.

This, however, is not the end of the action. A section which is called "The Finishing Song" in the Bassingham manuscript follows. It is really the continuation and completion of the wooing action which has been threading through the entire ceremony. The Song is in the form of a wooing dialogue between the Fool and the Lady. The Fool begins by singing of his love and promising Gold, Pearl, and "Rich costley Robes." The Lady scorns his offer and announces:

> I do never intend at all
> Not to be at any Young Man's call.[D]

At this the Fool rejects the Lady and says he will find "as handsome a fair one," as she. Now the Lady relents, begs the Fool to reconsider, which he hastily does. The action concludes with a dance between the Fool, the Lady and the Doctor.

There are two versions of the Bassingham Play, however, a Men's and a Children's. One might expect the Children's version to be shorter,

---

[c] In many versions this action leads to some fine, rowdy comic business as well as some pointed social satire in the folk idiom. In Laxton, Nottinghamshire, for instance, Dame Jane approaches Tom with her baby and he asks,

> Who told you to bring it here?
> DAME JANE: I went to the Office for the Poor
> And was told to bring it to the biggest
> fool I could find. And that's you!

J. W. Price, MS., Vaughan Williams Library Collection (n.d.). H.C., II, 347.

[D] Baskerville, 92–98. See below, p. 112, for the relationship between this kind of song and the Elizabethan jig.

omitting questionable actions like Dame Jane's paternity claim. This is not the case. The Children's version is, in fact, more extended and does include the appearance of Dame Jane with her doll and the paternity dialogue with the Fool.[E] It also continues past the wooing dialogue with one more action which is of enormous importance.

After the dance, the Fool steps forward and announces,

> I am come to invite you all to my wife's wedding: what you like best you must bring on with you. How should I no [*sic*] what everybody likes? Some likes fish, others likes flesh, but as for myself I like some good pottaty gruel, so what you like the best you must bring on with you.[4]

This is a fairly concise version of the invitation to the wedding feast. In some cases, it can go on for a full page, specifying, in nonsense figures, all the delicacies that the guests might like.[F] After the invitation in Bassingham, the Fool and the Lady sing, "We will have a jovel wedding," a traditional folk song which once again includes nonsense figures about the banquet fare.

> We'll have a lim of a lark and We'll have
> 　　louse to roast.
> We'll have a farthing leaf and cut a good
> 　　thumping toast.
> ri for laurel laddy ri for laurel lay.[5]

At the conclusion of the performance, the Fool leaves. The rest of the troupe sings, "Good Master and Mistress, now our Fool is gone," and follow him out in procession.

The shape and focus of the Bassingham Play can be considered representative of the whole type we call the Wooing Ceremony. Even at first glance certain qualities strike us which help serve to distinguish it from the Hero-Combat and Sword Ceremony. The first is the obvious importance of the wooing action itself and along with that, the necessary ap-

---

[E] When Chambers reproduced the Bassingham play in *The English Folk Play* (Oxford, 1933), pp. 92–98, he made a compilation of the two versions, indicating sections exclusively from the Children's Play by parentheses.

[F] Three examples of these extended invitations can be found in the versions from Broughton, Lincolnshire: Baskerville, p. 253; Kirton-in-Lindsay, Lincolnshire: Mabel Peacock, MS., Ordish Collection (n.d.); and Swinderby, Lincolnshire: Baskerville, p. 268.

pearance of at least one "female." The second is the sense of unity of action which is far greater here than in either of the other two types. The third is the apparent lack of interest in the combat, death and resurrection. The death and resurrection do appear in practically every version of the Wooing Ceremony,[G] but they are invariably treated in the same peremptory manner we have seen in Bassingham.

Once we have extricated the line of pure action from the Bassingham version, then, what we have is a play in which a Lady is wooed by a series of suitors. She rejects all of them until the Fool finally wins her. The Fool then invites the spectators to join the wedding ceremony. During the course of the wooing, the action is interrupted twice; first by the appearance of an old woman with a baby which she claims belongs to the Fool; second, by a combat in which one character dies and is brought back to life.

It is through this pure line of action that we can begin to move back farther than we have yet gone into the origin of the men's ceremonial.

Ritual Origins and Continental Analogues

A great deal has always been made of the ritual combat between winter and summer as the primitive basis of the men's ceremonial.[H] A direct, comparatively simple line of descent has, in fact, been generally assumed. Although the seasonal combat does, undoubtedly, contribute to the action, certain equally vital actions have been disregarded.

When scholars like Chambers and Beatty began dealing with the men's ceremonial in detail, they had at their disposal information primarily concerned with the Hero-Combat. Very few Wooing Plays were known and those that were available already showed strong literary influences at work on them.[I] It was logical, therefore, to consider the

[G] The texts from Broughton and Swinderby have no combat, although Broughton contains lines in the Ancient Man's wooing action which may indicate a combat. Baskerville, pp. 250–262.

In Winterton, Lincolnshire, combat boast fragments appear in the *quête*. Mabel Peacock, "Plough Monday Mummeries," *NQ,* 9th s., VII (April 27, 1901), 324.

[H] This is dealt with fully by Chambers in *The English Folk Play,* pp. 216ff., and in *The Medieval Stage,* I (Oxford, 1903), 206–248; T. F. Ordish, "English Folk Drama," *FL,* IV (1893), 159–160, deals specifically with the Hero-Combat's St. George as a summer figure.

[I] When Chambers published *The English Folk Play,* 1933, he cited nineteen

Hero-Combat the earliest prototype and the Wooing Play as either an atypical example of the Hero-Combat or a literary folk play, sentimental, artificial and only distantly related to the major form. For these early scholars, the combat was the crucial action of the dramatic ritual.

This was, to be sure, before the bulk of the Wooing Ceremony texts were collected and therefore before the significance of the findings of Wace and Dawkins on the mummers' plays of Thrace and the Balkans could be fully assimilated.[J] Nevertheless, even with only the Hero-Combat and the Sword Ceremony as the basic types, certain discrepancies in the theory of the strict winter-summer combat origin were overlooked. For instance, if the agonists of the Hero-Combat were the representatives of summer and winter, why, after summer was vanquished and magically reborn, was the pattern never completed? Why did not the summer figure destroy winter? What was to be made of the unrelated *quête* figures? Finally, what was to be made of the embarrassing absence of any combat at all in the majority of Sword Plays?

The answers to many of these questions become apparent if we consider the Wooing Ceremony the oldest form of men's ceremonial. If this is the case, the wooing action assumes hitherto unrecognized importance, while the combat is thrown into a new perspective against a much larger design. The conflict between summer and winter becomes only one of a number of mimetic actions all of which spring from the same common, affective purpose: fertility.

By the time we have it documented from the East Midlands, the wooing action is a fairly tame version of the processes of fertility. Nevertheless, there is evidence of its more primitive form from the continent. The mummers' plays of Northern Greece are far more sexually explicit than the "civilized" versions of Great Britain; but the correspondences between them are far too striking to be dismissed.

---

versions. In 1953, M. W. Barley, "Plough Plays in the East Midlands," *JEFDSS,* VII (December 1953), 91–95, was able to document eighty-nine. There are eighty-five listed in E. C. Cawte *et al., English Ritual Drama* (London, 1967).

[J] R. M. Dawkins, "The Modern Carnival in Thrace," *JHS,* XXVI (1906), 191–206; A. J. B. Wace, "North Greek Festivals," *BSA,* XVI (1909), 232–253; "Mumming Plays in the Southern Balkans," *BSA,* XIX (1912), 148–165. Although Chambers demonstrates an awareness of these findings (*English Folk Play,* pp. 233–235), it is puzzling that in *The Medieval Stage,* 1903, before the parallel between the wooing ceremony and the Balkan plays was available, he placed a greater emphasis on the ceremony than in the work of 1933.

In 1906, R. M. Dawkins published his descriptions of some mummers' plays he had witnessed in Northern Greece.[6] One of these, the Haghios Gheorghios play from Thrace is in the form of a luck-bringing perambulation. The procession is led by the two major actors, called *kalogheroi*. Both men wear goatskin masks which cover part of their faces and sheep bells tied around their waists and ankles. Their shoulders are padded and their faces and hands are blackened with ashes. One of the *kalogheroi* carries a phallus and one a cross bow. Following them come two boys who will later be the "brides" of the ritual, then a Babo, or old woman who carries a basket representing a cradle. Inside the basket is a doll wrapped in rags. Next come two gypsies with ash-blackened hands, carrying scourging rods and, finally, several more players carrying rods and whips. As the procession moves past certain houses, the Babo and the gypsies perform obscene pantomimes of copulation.

The action begins with a mime in which the Babo and the two gypsies forge a ploughshare. We see them build a fire and beat out the metal for it. After this, the rag doll is taken from the cradle. It grows up into the phallus-bearing *kalogheros* who develops a voracious appetite, demanding more and more food, and then calls for a bride. He is married to one of the boy-brides. After the marriage, the second *kalogheros* enters with his cross-bow. There is a fight. The phallus-bearer is killed. The bride laments and after a pause the victim revives. No doctor appears here. At the resurrection of the phallus-bearer, the completed plough is brought into the dancing circle. This is drawn by all the characters; seeds are scattered behind it and there is a general cry for good crops.

A similar play occurs in Thessaly where twelve dancers, including a groom who wears bells around his waist similar to those of the morris dancers, go from house to house.[K] There is also an Arab or Moor with blackened face and sheepskin mask and a tail, a Bride, and a Doctor. The structure of the Thessalian action includes a dispute over the bride, the death of the groom, the call for the doctor and the cure. Here, too, the obscene sexual pantomime is an integral part of the proceedings as well as an antiphonal chorus.[L]

[K] In a series of exquisite costume renderings by Alison Helm which trace the changes in the men's ceremonial costume, this similarity is made strikingly clear. H.C.

[L] Wace, "Mumming Plays," reports on similar ceremonies from Macedonia, while Dawkins has recorded still others in his study. Theodor Gaster, *Thespis*

The essential characteristics of all the Balkan versions are the Bride, the groom, the interloper, the old woman with the baby, often an old man as well, and a death and resurrection. These, of course, are precisely the characteristics of the English Wooing Ceremony. In both cases the marriage is established between the "Female" and the leader of the procession, the Fool in Great Britain and the phallus-bearing *kalogheros* in Greece. This helps to substantiate our contention that the ribald clown as we know him in the Greatham Sword Dance, the club-bearing *quêteur* of the Hero-Combat, the Fool of the Wooing Ceremony and the ancient *phallophoroi* derive from the same ritual figure.

The action, too, is analogous. The Greek plays, however, are more unified than the English. Because of this, they help clarify some important aspects of the ceremony. One of the disturbing elements of the English Wooing Ceremony is the apparently arbitrary split between the combat and the wooing action. The evidence from Greece points to the connection. In both the English and the Greek examples, the major conflict is over the possession of the female. It is from this conflict that the combat springs in Greece.[M] It is as a direct consequence of the wooing action, then, that the male fertility figure, the phallus-bearer, dies and is reborn. The major conflict in the English play is also found in the wooing action. It seems most likely that at one time the death of the male fertility figure here, too, sprang directly from the wooing and that it is only through gradual fragmentation that the two elements have become separate entities.

What all this certainly implies is that we have in the wooing play a ceremony, first and foremost, of fertility, whether it is expressed on the magical human level of copulation, the agricultural level exemplified in the dragging of the plough and the scattering of the seeds, or the cosmic level played out in the combat of the seasons. In the Wooing Ceremony, whether of England, Thrace, or Thessaly, we see all these elements brought together in their most coherent form.

(New York, 1961), pp. 406–435, discusses an ancient Near Eastern burlesque fragment. This is "The Canaanite Poem of the Gracious Gods," which includes much ribald play, pantomimes of copulation, two brides, the birth of "the gracious gods" with abnormally voracious appetites.

The Rumanian Kalusari play, too, bears a strong resemblance to the Balkan mummers. See Appendix G.

[M] This is true, also, of the Rumanian Kalusari play. See Appendix F.

The Corn Spirit

There are two further events which must be considered in connection with the fertility purpose of the Wooing Ceremony: the appearance of the Old Woman and the Fool's invitation to the wedding.

Sir James Frazer gives us an insight into the figure of the Old Woman in his discussion of the corn spirit in *The Golden Bough*.[7] After dealing with the personification of the spirit of vegetation in double form as male and female in various cultures, he proceeds to describe its appearance in "a double female form as both old and young."[8] In connection with this, Frazer describes a Scottish custom of fashioning two female figures out of the reaped corn. These figures are called the Corn Maiden and the Old Wife, or *cailleach*.[N] The Maiden is invariably fashioned from the last stalks left standing while the Old Wife is often made from earlier cuts. The Corn Maiden is retained by the farmer all year, but as soon as he is finished with his own field, he passes the Old Wife on to a slower neighbor.

> Thus while each farmer keeps his own Maiden, as the embodiment of the young and fruitful spirit of the corn, he passes on the Old Wife as soon as he can to a neighbor, and so the old lady may make the rounds of all the farms in the district before she finds a place in which to lay her venerable head.[9]

Wherever this double-female form appears, the Old Wife represents the corn spirit of the past year, while the Maiden signifies the present, fruitful time. It is natural, then, that the old, dying figure should be rejected in favor of the young and fruitful one.

This, of course, is what we find in the action of the Wooing Ceremony. The double-female figure appears here as the Lady and Old Dame Jane. The Fool woos the young female. Old Dame Jane arrives with the infant in her arms giving evidence that the Fool has already wooed and won her. She tells how she has been flitting "hither and thither over the meadows," until now she is a "down old widow," and tells the Fool to take his child. But the Fool rejects her in favor of the young corn

---

[N] In Pembrokeshire she is called the Hag.

spirit, just as the farmer has retained the Maiden and passed the Old Wife on to his neighbor.[o]

The Babo of the Balkans, too, can be seen as the previous year's corn spirit, for it is the infant she carries with her who grows into the phallus-bearing *kalogheros* during the course of the play and marries the young bride. The old corn spirit has thus given life to the husband of the new.

The Sacred Wedding

The action does not end with the rejection of the old corn spirit in England, however, nor does it end with the growth of the *kalogheros* in the Balkans. There is yet another mimetic action to be performed and this, once again, is essential to the magical nature of the ceremony in terms of fertility. In England the Fool has still to win the Lady; in Greece the *kalogheros* must marry the Bride. There is still the "sacred marriage" to be performed.

F. M. Cornford deals with this element of primitive ritual in *The Origin of Attic Comedy*. He explains that in a sacred marriage the bridegroom and the bride are representatives of divine or spiritual beings, containing within them some form of the powers of fertility in nature;

> their object, which is to promote fertility of all kinds, is effected by the methods of mimetic (sympathetic) magic; a sexual union is consummated or feigned in order that all natural powers of fertility may be stimulated to perform their function and give increase of crops and herds and of man himself.[10]

He then goes on to compare the ritual marriage with the mythic marriage of Zeus and Demeter at Eleusis and Zeus and Hera elsewhere.[p] In these cases, however, the divinities have already reached the fully anthro-

---

[o] As far as I know, this connection between the two female figures of the corn spirit and the two women of the Wooing Ceremony has not been noted before. Margaret Dean-Smith, "The Life Cycle," *FL*, LXIX (1958), 237–238, deals with the Old Woman and the Ancient Man, who also occasionally appears as a wooer, the Fool and the Lady, and the infant as representatives of the three stages of the life cycle. I do not believe my theory is incompatible with this since both recognize the ritual of fertility as the source of the play.

[p] The analogy with Zeus and Demeter is of particular interest, for in another context Demeter and Persphone can be seen to comprise a mythic version of the double-female corn spirit.

pomorphic stage of development. Prior to that, there is evidence of figures taking the form of animals such as the bull, the goat or the ram. "In other instances," Cornford goes on," the spirit of fertility may be Dionysus himself, or the vaguer figure of Phales, who is little more than the emblem of human procreation, the *phallus*, personified." This leads to his conclusion that even by the time the ritual has turned distinctly into drama with Aristophanic comedy, the protagonist is still found wearing an artificial phallus.[11]

Both these observations, the previous animal nature of the divine bridegroom in the sacred marriage and the presence of the phallus, find correspondents in Greece and England. They may account for the presence of the tail on the Thessalian *kalogheroi* and the phallus that is carried in Thrace. In England, too, an animal's tail is a common feature of the Wooing Ceremony costume [Q] and from Yorkshire, in 1793, we have some lines recollected from the childhood of John Jackson which, interestingly enough, point to both the animal nature of the Fool and the sacred marriage.

> My name it is Captain Calf-tail, Calf-tail,
> And on my back it is plain to be seen;
> Although I'm simple and wear a fool's cap,
> I'm dearly beloved of a queen.[R]

This leads us into the final element of the Fool's invitation to the banquet.

Once again we may look to the cultural anthropologists for our clues to the significance of the action. Cornford, Frazer, and Theodor Gaster all deal with the concept of the communal feast as an integral part of the fertility ceremony.

In Cornford's analysis of Aristophanic comedy, the Sacrifice and Feast come between Agon and the Marriage. Cornford is able to discern a direct connection between the sacrificial feast and the death and resur-

---

[Q] It is interesting, too, that in many villages the players are called "plough bullocks." Considered as a form of animal disguise, this feature can also account for the frequent appearance of the hobby horse in all types of the men's ceremonial.

[R] John Jackson, *The History of the Scottish Stage* (Edinburgh, 1793), pp. 410–411. The entire reference to this performance offers an insight into the interaction between literary sources and ceremonial figures from all three types such as the Calling-on of the Sword Play, the wooing, the combat, the death and resurrection. See Appendix I.

rection. He first speaks of the traces of ancient ritual in which it is the fertility god himself who is the victim, whether in his earlier, totemistic form as an animal or in his later, anthropomorphic form as man.

> He is dismembered and the pieces of his body are either devoured raw in a savage omophagy, or cooked and eaten in a sacramental feast. Or again, in yet simpler forms, the fragments of the divine body are distributed among the worshippers to be placed in stall and manger, or strewn upon the fields for the fertilization of the crops. In all these cases, the fundamental need is the same; the essential purpose is that of the phallic rites, which aim at spreading the benign influence as widely as possible, so that all members of the community may have their share.[12]

These pieces later become grain, "given to the worshippers to be used for spreading the beneficent influence of the fertility rite throughout the community." This portion of the ancient phallic ritual corresponds precisely to the scattering of the grain we have already seen in Thrace and the dispensing of luck throughout the community through the perambulation of the ploughboys. We see a reference to this kind of communal feast as well as the scattering of the grain in the sacrifice scene of Aristophanes' *Peace,* in which Trygaeus orders Xanthias to take barley grains from the basket and throw some of them to the spectators.

But we find this concept of the communal feast even more clearly and consistently expressed at the conclusion of Aristophanic comedy with the final banquet, marriage celebration or invitation to the feast. In the Wooing Ceremony itself, the Fool's invitation to the community to partake of the feast is directly related. Although it is seen in its clearest form in the Wooing Play, the communal feast is by no means limited to that form of the men's ceremonial. We have already seen it alluded to in the sacrament of the Buophonia which informs the Sword Play and the *quête* figures of the Hero-Combat which call for food and drink for all.[8]

Frazer tells us of the variations of the Sacrament of the First Fruits

---

[8] Cornford, p. 44, finds an even more specific analogy between the Cook of Aristophanic comedy and the Doctor of folk drama both of whom are life-restorers. In Aristophanes' *Knights,* for instance, the sausage-seller effects the rejuvenation of Demos, the old judge, by boiling him. Cornford says, "A cook who can perform such miraculous operations is manifestly a magician, and his profession coalesces with that of the Doctor in the primitive functions of the medicine-man—a figure who, as we shall see later, stands out in the dim past behind the Doctor who revives the slain in the folk plays."

in primitive cultures in which the "divine essence" of the spirit of fertility is absorbed by eating the corn spirit in cakes.[13] This is also the basis of English soul-caking in which the spirits of the departed are said to be contained in the "soul-cakes" which are brought from house to house in a luck-bringing perambulation on All Soul's Eve. The Souling Play, which is a popular form of the Hero-Combat in Cheshire is performed as part of this ritual. Here, again, the sense of the communal feast is strong and helps further to connect the ceremonial with the fertility of the land in the coming season.

What all these analogies suggest, simply, is that the Wooing Ceremony from the East Midlands is the form of the men's ceremonial closest in structure and thematic focus to its primitive ancestor, the fertility ritual. It would be folly to try to reconstruct that ritual with any kind of certainty, but from the evidence of the Balkan, Thracian, and Thessalian plays we can discern elements which point to the validity of this theory.

The Later Development

Beginning with the fertility ceremony, then, we can follow certain clues which will allow us to trace the development of this most primitive performance into its modern form as a seasonal folk drama. It is in this process that we can most clearly see the operation of specific literary influences, particularly the folk wooing song and the Elizabethan jig.

These, however, do not enter clearly until the beginning of the sixteenth century. Up to that time we are on less safe ground and can only assume that the ritual, which originally bore a close resemblance to its Balkan counterparts, underwent alterations with the advent of Christianity and the various changes in the social structure of the country.

In Greece, the phallic song finally attained qualities of unequalled brilliance, invention, and intellectual wit in the comedies of Aristophanes. In England this development was not attained, although there are faint traces of satiric social comment in some plays, particularly late examples.

Christianity was probably one important reason for this. There are numerous examples of the conflict between Christian and pagan practices in England in the early years of Christianity. The policy of the church in regard to these was generally one of canny assimilation. Whatever could be salvaged from the old magical beliefs was redefined and set to work for an easier transition to the new religion. The use of ancient sacred wells and groves for church sites is only one example.[T] The transformation of agricultural fertility festivals into seasonal Christian celebrations is another. Parts of the medieval mystery cycles spring from this process, too. The processional nature of the performances, the coarse burlesque and the appearance of comic devils, complete with tails and clubs owe much to their popularity in the primitive fertility ceremony.[U]

But with the rise of Christianity, and a specifically Christian drama, the men's ceremonial lost its force. It was probably the rise of the Christian drama as the expression and celebration of the people's religious experience which cut off any possibility for the development of the primitive ceremony into anything like the strength of Attic comedy.

By the time we reach the sixteenth century, we can begin to find the direct influences of wooing songs, jigs and even whole scenes from plays. All these forms were available to the people of even the most remote villages through feasts and fairs at which travelling players and balladmongers were a common diversion. In *The Elizabethan Jig,* Baskerville says,

> The framework of the mummers' wooing plays . . . had its basis in pagan rituals, but doubtless much of the dialogue and even some whole scenes resulted from the combination of this ritual with early wooing songs no longer extant, the whole being modified from time to time by new borrowings. There are numerous parallel passages in the wooing plays and ballads that seem to represent conventional phraseology, and it is often a question whether the plays themselves influenced the extant ballads or were influenced by earlier versions of the ballad dialogues in which a clown or farming man woos a scornful lady. From the latter part of the sixteenth century on, there is undoubted evidence that the folk plays borrowed from songs, jigs and plays, probably as performed in feasts, wakes and fairs.[14]

Two examples of this kind of influence will suffice.

In the Swinderby Play there are three distinct wooing actions. In the

[T] See, for instance, Chambers, *Medieval Stage,* I, 95–96, for a letter from Gregory the Great to Ethelbert of Kent in the year 601; see also, Felix Grendon, "The Anglo-Saxon Charms," *JAF,* XXII (April 1909), 110; and Baskerville, "Dramatic Aspects," 61.

[U] T. F. Ordish, "Folk Drama," *FL,* II (1891), 314–335, and "English Folk Drama," *FL,* IV (1893), 149–175, held the belief that it was the Christian drama which diverted the stream of folk ritual into less rich soil.

third, the Husbandman tries to win the Lady with a version of the folk song, "Madam I have gold and silver." But the sequence following has even more specific references. Baskerville points out the close resemblance between this section of the play and the ballad, "Young Roger of the Mill." [15] Although it is impossible to ascertain any specific dates for either the ballad or the play, there is little doubt that "Young Roger of the Mill" in the form we have it here was grafted on to the play rather than taken from it. The most potent reason for believing this is that by the time we reach this section in Swinderby, the typical wooing action has already been completed with the Fool's winning of the Lady. The third wooing is an embellishment, introduced for entertainment and using a popular ballad of the period.

We see an even more blatant example of this kind of embellishment in the Broughton Play. [16] This version begins with a conventional prologue by the Fool, who calls himself "Noble Anthony." The Lady enters and introduces herself, telling of the time she was a "maid in blooming years," and instead of a man, met with a clown. Quite suddenly, however, the conventional action gives way to a dialogue between the Fool and the First Ribboner. This is a thoroughly incoherent exchange which would have no meaning at all were it not for the fact that, even in its garbled form, it corresponds to the dialogue of the Induction to *Wily Beguiled,* a comedy of 1606. [17] One might suspect that both the Broughton Play and the farce draw from some common source, but the words themselves deal so specifically with theatrical terms that they leave little doubt as to the precedence of the literary play and its direct influence on the folk ceremony. We need only compare one short passage to see this. At the opening of *Wily Beguiled,* the Prologue says:

> Where are these paltrie plaiers? stil poaring in their papers and never perfect? for shame come forth, your Audience stay so long, their eies dim with expectation. [18]

In Broughton, the speech is transformed into

> wher's all this paltry poor; still paltry in this place, and yet not perfect for shame, step forth people's eyes looks dim with a very red expectation. [v]

[v] Baskerville, "Mummers' Wooing Plays," 250. In *The Elizabethan Jig,* p. 251, he also cites sections of Cox's pastoral droll, *Diphilo and Granida,* in the Somersetshire play.

One other factor contributing to the evolution of the Wooing Ceremony as we know it today is that of social change. We can see the beginnings of this with the multiplication of wooers that seems to occur, the way they are particularized and made to reflect the organization of the society and the sympathies of the folk. This accounts for the appearance of figures like the Squire, the Farmer's Eldest Son, the Knight, and the Lawyer as common wooers.

The Recruiting Sergeant

Social comment also accounts for a figure who brings with him an entirely new action, one which becomes an integral part of the play in many villages. This is the figure of the Recruiting Sergeant. There are at least fifty-nine versions of the Wooing Play which include the Recruiting Sergeant as a principal figure. Often he is one of the combatants. From the frequency of his appearance and the similarity of language and actions from version to version, it is also likely that there is a lost literary source at work here, either a jig or a play.[w] One would suspect it is a jig since the action is a rather short, complete one, involving two men and a woman, who sing most of their lines.

A play, reprinted by Baskerville under the title of "The Recruiting Sergeant," will show how this figure is assimilated into the basic structure of the ceremony. This play might come from somewhere in the vicinity of Broughton since it begins with the same borrowings from *Wily Beguiled,* including the short prologue in which the Fool introduces himself as "Noble Anthony, as melancholy as a mantle tree," the Lady follows with her history as a "maid in blooming years" and the Fool garbles the Induction speech calling for the players to come forth.

After this the Sergeant makes his appearance, announcing his orders to "enlist all that follow the Cart or the plow." The Fool and the Sergeant then pursue a comic dialogue in which the Fool says he has come to see the Sergeant dance and sing. This short passage is of particular interest for it takes the precise form of the Sword Ceremonies, giving us

---

[w] A short jig appearing in D'Urfey's *Pills to Purge Melancholy,* v (London, 1719), 319–321, has the tone of the Wooing Ceremony's Recruiting Sergeant action, but there is no actual parallel between the two except in the call for recruits. See also George Farquhar's *The Recruiting Officer* for a delightful treatment of this same common situation in the professional theater.

yet another link between the different types of ceremony (see above, p. 75). This part of the Recruiting action breaks off suddenly when the Second Ribboner challenges the Recruiting Sergeant, calling himself a "champion bold," and declaims figures from St. George's typical history boast. The Sergeant gives the counter-challenge, but instead of a combat this action ends in a dance.

Now the full recruiting action picks up with the Young Man, the Sergeant and the Lady. The Young Man is in despair because the Lady has rejected his advances. The Sergeant tries to cheer him up and gets him to enlist. The Lady laments, but the Sergeant tells her the young man would have probably left her anyway. The Lady decides against the recruit again. In many versions, the Sergeant then proceeds to woo the Lady himself, which is the kind of action one would expect in a jig. Here, however, the Fool steps in immediately and wins the Lady with a wooing song which is followed by the Recruiting Sergeant's common verse,

> Come my lads that has a mind for listing,
>   Come and go along with me
> You shall have all kinds of liquers
>   When you list in Company
>
> And ten Guineas then shall be your Bounty
>   if along with me you will go.
> You hat shall be so neatly dressed
>   and we will cut a gallant show.[19]

The normal wooing actions resume with the appearance of Dame Jane, her bastard child and an Ancient Man who woos the Lady and is rejected.

By the eighteenth century, this figure of the Recruiting Sergeant and his action which includes the rejected suitor and the Lady have become an integral part of the play. It was during this time that the practice of recruiting ploughboys for the Queen's service was common. Whether the figure of the Recruiting Sergeant came from a literary source or not, it is likely that the reason for his adoption into so many versions of the play, and his ability to maintain his position as a central figure, was his familiarity in the lives of the people.

The Wooing Ceremony as a type of the men's ceremonial affords us the clearest line of evolution from primitive fertility to seasonal folk drama. The late versions which we have documented represent a stage in which any concept of the play as a genuine magical force has dissipated. What remains is a seasonal entertainment of enormous flexibility, open to any kind of embellishment, reworking, restructuring that the players see fit to impose upon it. Nevertheless, what is so impressive is not so much the range of forms the play demonstrates in this complex history, but its ability to remain so extraordinarily coherent and unified.

Having established the Wooing Ceremony as the type of men's ceremonial closest to the primitive origins of all three types, we must now look briefly at how the Hero-Combat and the Sword Ceremony derive from that ritual, and deal with just what this whole process can tell us about the nature of the folk drama in terms of its ritual origins.

SIX

TRACES OF ANCIENT MYSTERY

Throughout our examination of the texts of the ceremonies we have been looking at any number of primitive rituals for analogous actions and possible explanations and insights into the origins and development of the particular types. It is time, now, to synthesize these observations.

The work of scholars such as Harrison, Cornford, Murray, and Gaster dealing with the development of drama out of ritual are well known. It might be valuable, however, to review briefly the major lines of the process before we apply them to the development of the English men's ceremonial.

Myth, Ritual, and Drama

In Chapter Three we characterized ritual as pure action and drama as explained action. By pure action we meant, simply, man doing. In ritual the action is not necessarily interpretative as it is in drama; it is magical and directly purposive. Its purpose is to insure the revitalization of man's immediate world, and it is this direct, effective purpose which defines ritual and renders it distinct from drama. It has been suggested that Macbeth contains all the elements of the archetypal winter king who must be slain by the figure of summer.[1] This is a splendid insight, but no one would seriously think of performing the tragedy in order to insure a punctual thaw. Ritual is performed for precisely that kind of reason.[A]

[A] For the sake of clarity, it should be noted that the crucial distinction between the concepts of ritual and drama lies in their purpose rather than the

Theodor Gaster divides ritual into two types, *kenosis,* or emptying, and *plerosis,* or filling.[2] The alternation of these two types corresponds to the rhythm of the cosmos, the constant evacuation of the life of the earth and its replenishment with the changing of the seasons, the rising and setting of the sun, the animal processes of sleeping and waking, death and birth. The rites of *plerosis* include "mock combats against the forces of drought or evil, mass mating, the performance of rain charms and the like, all designed to effect the reinvigoration of the topocosm." [3]

Now, as religious consciousness changes, so does the nature of ritual. These changes complicate the problem of tracing any kind of drama back to its ritual antecedents. Ritual obviously did not shade into drama at one late point and then fall out of existence like some unused appendage. Religious ritual has always continued to develop even while great periods of drama flourished. The Greeks perpetuated serious religious observances while Aeschylus, Sophocles, and Euripides wrote their plays. Pure ritual actions like the Dionysiac procession were, in fact, performed as preludes to the performances of the plays themselves in Greece. The medieval mystery cycles may have grown out of the church service, but even at the height of their achievement they only complemented Christian ritual; they never supplanted it.

What becomes clear as we learn more and more about the nature of the relationship between ritual, myth, and drama is that the last two forms are latent in all forms of religious consciousness and can develop and come to fruition at any time. Indeed, the three can never be totally separated. We are trying to separate the different forms here only in order to have some defined concepts with which to work. In operation, the three concepts are interdependent, with variations only in emphasis.

This idea that myth and drama can develop and become the predominant expression of any form of religious consciousness is, I believe, precisely what accounts for the distinction among the three types of the English men's ceremonial as well as their underlying unity in the death and resurrection motif. Each of the three types originates in the same basic rite of *plerosis,* but each emerges from a different form of that rite.

In her brilliant study, *Themis,* Jane Ellen Harrison traces the develop-

---

presence or absence of spoken language. As we saw in the discussion of the Anglo-Saxon charms, above, pp. 56–58, words can be used as effective tools in precisely the way movement can.

ment of Greek religion through its various early stages.[B] In using Miss Harrison's outline of the development of Greek religion to define these forms of religious consciousness, it must be thoroughly understood that we are not trying to establish any direct relationship between the three types of English men's ceremonial and the Greek culture. Harrison's study affords us an extraordinarily clear, concise picture of the evolving stages of one religion. It also affords us a vocabulary with which to define what appear to be archetypes of religious consciousness. Our theory is that the three types of English men's ceremonial are representative dramatic crystallizations of the rituals of three different religious attitudes similar to those of the Greeks.

Harrison begins with a concept of collective action or emotion as exemplified in the Rite of Thunder and the Omophagia. The Rite of Thunder focuses attention on the non-physical forces variously called *Mana, Orenda,* and *wa-ko-nida.* These are unarticulated, invisible forces which are believed to pervade all life, binding them together in a common existence. They are the abstract spirit powers which precede the divinities.[4]

With the Omophagia, we have an example of collective action. It is a totemistic form of religious expression. The totemistic ritual is based on the consciousness of the relation of a unified group to another non-human group through the agency of a common Mana, and takes the form of a sacrament or communal feast. The totemistic ceremony is invariably *methektic* rather than *mimetic;* that is, it is the expression of participation in a common nature between man and non-human rather than the imitation of alien characteristics. The Omophagia, or communal meal, is an example of the totemistic ceremony, as is the Buophonia, which we discussed in relation to the Sword Ceremony.

As religious consciousness changes, a sense of the differences between

---

[B] Jane Ellen Harrison, *Themis* (Cambridge, 1912), *passim.* In this study Miss Harrison deals primarily with the phase preceding the concept of the anthropomorphic gods as we find it in the Olympians. Gilbert Murray acknowledges his debt to Harrison when he takes this study further and traces the development of the Olympian deities in *Four Stages of Greek Religion* (New York, 1912), and in the later, expanded *Five Stages of Greek Religion* (New York, 1925). See also, Harrison's earlier study, *Prolegomena to the Study of Greek Religion* (Cambridge, 1908) and Herbert Weisinger's later use of her findings in *Tragedy and the Paradox of the Fortunate Fall* (London, 1953), pp. 117ff.

the group and the totem may grow. Consciousness of the distinction between individuals may grow as well. The responsibility for the performance of the rites shifts from the entire community to a specialized group and finally to a single figure endowed with the potency to effect the regeneration of the land and the tribe by his own ritual actions.^c Along with this, the concept of the divinities becomes expressed more and more in human terms. Here we have the figure of the Hero-*daimon* who dies and is reborn for the perpetuation of the community. When the consciousness of the distinction between the individuals of the community is fully established, the familiar rituals of the scapegoat and the heroic combat, like Frazer's famous challenge at Nemi, occur.^D

As long as these actions retain a direct, immediate purpose and are believed to effect some change in man's environment, they retain the nature of pure ritual.

Myth, on the other hand, is interpretative. It translates the immediate, functional purpose of ritual into ideal, permanent terms. This relationship of myth to ritual is most clearly and concisely expressed by Gaster. "Seasonal *rituals* are functional in character," he says.

> Their purpose is periodically to revive the topocosm, that is, the entire complex of any given locality conceived as a living organism. But this topocosm possesses both a punctual and a durative aspect, representing, not only the actual and present community, but also that ideal and continuous entity of which the latter is but the current manifestation. Accordingly, seasonal rituals are accompanied by *myths* which are designed to present the purely functional acts in terms of ideal and durative situations.[5]

Harrison shows how the responsibility for ritual action tends to shift from the community to the individual in Greek religion until all magical power is invested in the figure of the king.^E This is on the plane of

---

^c This process of gradual individualizing and symbolic separation can also be seen to operate on the level of individual consciousness. See, for instance, Erich Neumann, *The Origins and History of Consciousness* (New York, 1954), *passim.*

^D See also Weisinger's investigation of this concept in the Ancient Near East, Judaism, and Christianity in *Tragedy and The Paradox of the Fortunate Fall,* pp. 44–11, 132–221.

^E This is treated fully by Frazer, pp. 31–168. See also, Samuel H. Hooke, ed., *Myth, Ritual and Kingship* (Oxford, 1958).

man's "punctual" world, as Gaster characterizes it. But this same figure has his counterpart on the "durative" plane. That is the figure of the god. And the actions of that god at his own level of operation are both an ideal reflection and an explanation of man's action in ritual. The god, then, is the permanent, mythic archetype for the temporary, ritualistic figure of the individual king.

Granting this concept of the relationship between myth and ritual, it is not difficult to see how myth is coexistent with the ritual of all periods of religious development. As soon as man generalizes his actions, as soon as he becomes conscious of a pattern and rhythm of existence, myth is manifested.

Therefore, if man acts only in order to achieve an immediate, temporal result he is performing "pure" ritual. If that action becomes a conscious imitation of the mythic action, if it begins to explain the immediate in terms of the ideal, drama has been born. The performer is no longer simply acting; he is conscious of re-enacting, as well. He is not only performing an action, he is imitating one. And as the element of drama becomes more refined, the action becomes less effective in concept and more imitative and explanatory. The idea of performing a task "in order to" is supplanted by the idea of performing it "as if."

Armed with information from our study of the texts as a guide to the nature of the action, we can now look at the three separate types of English men's ceremonial and see how they reflect the emergence of drama from three separate phases of religious development.[F]

The Sword Ceremony: Totemism

The Sword Ceremony most clearly reflects the totemistic form of religious celebration. The formal components such as the community slay-

[F] Arthur Beatty, "The St. George or Mummers' Play," *TWAS,* xv (October 1906), 323–324, was the first to see the direct connection between myth, ritual, and the development of the English Men's Ceremonial, although he focused exclusively on the Hero-Combat. "In nearly all the savage ceremonies," he says, "we see a very close connection between ceremony and myth, and there seems to be little doubt that the ceremony is not the derived form. In other words, the myth or legend is a late invention to explain the ceremony. In all cases where both survive, the ceremony has all the marks of being the original. Thus the legends, epics, and ritual songs have as their ancestor the pantomimic ceremony, and therefore we are not making an impossible or even an improbable assumption when we trace our mummers' play back to a mimetic ceremony."

ing, the repudiation, and the choral song connect, by analogy at least, with the totemistic Buophonia. Verbal elements like the Earsdon allusion to the slaying of the ox and the distribution of his flesh echo its sacramental nature. Until the dancers begin to take on the names of heroes or representatives of figures from the social structure, they are an anomalous group. The sense of representation of discrete figures or symbols is significantly absent. Although it is not a total community action such as the Mascarade of La Soule or the Archetringle of Laupen, Switzerland, ceremonies which have probably originated in a similar Rite of Plerosis, neither is it as articulated as the Wooing Ceremony or the Hero-Combat.[6] The underlying religious concept of the action appears to be one of a unified community identity rather than a society of individual worshipers.

The Wooing Ceremony: The Fertility-Daimon

The Wooing Ceremony and the Hero-Combat, on the other hand, both appear to spring from a ritual in which there is a sense of the distinction between human and non-human, between individual and individual.

There are two spring rituals from the old Roman year which can do

[6] The communal, undifferentiated nature of the Mascarade is attested to by the fact that the major performing units are two companies, the Reds and the Blacks. The Reds, or "Beautifuls," are the finest dancers. A few of these are individualized, but even the nature of their differentiation betrays totemistic origins, for the character of the *Zamalzain* is a hobby-horse, the Gherrero, or sweeper, is literally a "pig-man" and the *Gatuzain,* or Fool, literally a "cat-man." In the second part of the ceremony, the Mascarade becomes sacramental. Two gelders from the community of Blacks enter the circle and perform a burlesque dance. The horse joins them. The horse is shod and gelded. He sinks down, then, supported by his captors, staggers around the circle. At a given moment his forces suddenly return. He executes a series of leaps which become so prodigious that his last is a veritable hoisting, similar to the hoisting of the fool in Germanic sword dances.

The Archetringle on New Year's Eve consists of a "horde of terrifyingly masked figures in skins with enormous cow-like bells round their waists and long sticks in their hands who rush wildly about but neither dance nor act a play." Like the Mascarade dancers they are divided into two groups, *schöne* and *schieche.* The *schöne* are orderly, neat, handsomely dresed in ribbons, bells and tall crowns. The *schieche* are unruly, dirty, dressed in rags, masked with grotesque, distorted faces, and hung about with rats, mice, chains, and cowbells.

Both of these descriptions appear in Violet Alford and Rodney Gallop, *The Traditional Dance* (London, 1935), pp. 186–195, 179.

much to illuminate the development of the Wooing Ceremony for us. These are the rituals of the Mamuralia and Anna Perenna of March 14 and 15. March 15 was the day of the first full moon of the new year. On the day before, a man dressed in goat skins was led in procession through the streets of Rome, beaten with long white rods, and driven out of the city. This was Mamurius or Veturius, the embodiment of the Old Year, the Old Mars, Death, Winter driven out before the incoming New Year, the young Mars, Spring.[6] On the following day, the festival of Anna Perenna was held and it is here that we can see most clearly the kind of seasonal ritual from which the Wooing Ceremony may have sprung.

Harrison describes the Anna Perenna as simply "a rude drinking bout of the plebs; men and women revelled together, some in the open Campus Martius, others in rough huts made of sticks and branches; they sang and danced and prayed for as many years of life as they could drink cups of wine. It was just an ordinary New Year's festival." [7]

But Ovid tells a story in his *Fasti* which is the mythic explanation of the festival of Anna Perenna. Mars wishes to marry. He asks Anna to help him have Minerva, but old Anna veils her face and takes the place of the bride. Old Anna comes to Mars instead of his promised bride and he does not realize the deception. Fortunately, the veil is stripped away and Old Anna is discovered before the marriage is consummated. She is rejected just as Dame Jane is rejected in the Wooing Ceremony.[H]

Both of these rituals indicate a form of religious consciousness quite different from totemism. The mythic figures are anthropomorphic. The Mamuralia is basically a scapegoat ritual in which evil is embodied in a single figure and driven out. Ovid's story of the Anna Perenna conceives of the god as a fertility-*daimon*, a human symbol for the process of decay, death, and revival. Newborn and capable of rejuvenating the earth through divine marriage, he is the projection of collective emotion individualized.

Introducing Ovid's account, Harrison says that the story "may reflect a bit of rustic ritual." [8] Indeed it does, for it contains actions directly analagous to the English Wooing Ceremony as well as the Thracian and

<hr/>

[H] Sir James George Frazer, trans. *Ovid's Fasti* (London, 1931), pp. 169–171. In his Appendix, p. 397, Frazer makes a strong case for Mars as a fertility god, citing Cato the Elder's treatise on farming in which Mars is prayed to for the prosperity of the earth.

Balkan mummers' plays with the appearance of the old woman, her rejection by the bridegroom and the divine marriage. Even the scapegoat ritual of the Mamuralia finds its counterpart in the rejection of the old man by the young lady who is to be the bride.

The Hero-Combat: St. George as Hero-Daimon

The focus of the Hero-Combat type is on the individual combatants. The concept of the mythic figures portrayed has undergone another crucial transformation. In the form of religion reflected in the Wooing Ceremony, the fertility-*daimon* is conceived as a human with divine attributes. His marriage is responsible for the fertility of all the earth. In yet another form of the ritual the concept of the Hero, an even more highly individualized figure, predominates. The angle of vision shifts. The human figure endowed with divine attributes becomes simply the human figure of the dead ancestor, often a king who is responsible for, and representative of, the permanent life of the group. He is still a projection of the group consciousness, but in the examples of ritual like the Oschophoria with its coexistent myth the re-enactment of his death and resurrection becomes most clearly representational. The principal factors of the festival of the Oschophoria are the *agon* or contest, the *pathos,* a defeat or death, and the triumphant reappearance or rebirth. These are, of course, the principal factors of the Hero-Combat as well. It is interesting to note, too, that it is the Hero-Combat which has the closest analagous relation to the Greek drama, with the sequence of *Agon, Pathos, Threnos, Anagnorisis,* and *Theophany.*[1]

It is not unusual that the figure of St. George should play a role similar to that of the Hero-*Daimon* in the English Hero-Combat play. He was, first of all, the warrior saint. But beyond that, the pattern of his apocryphal legend coincides with the myth of the dying and reviving god. The story which is told in the Hero-Combat play is not that of his combat

[1] Harrison, *Themis,* pp. 260–363, prefaces her analysis of the Hero figure with a most concise discussion of Ridgeway's theory that agonistic festivals and drama alike find their origins not in magical ceremony but in funeral ceremonies at the grave of some historic individual. In Ridgeway's analysis totemism, vegetation spirits and the concept of the fertility-*daimon* are relegated to the position of secondary phenomena. For the full study of this approach, see William Ridgeway, *The Origin of Tragedy* (Cambridge, 1910), and *The Dramas and Dramatic Rituals of Non-European Races* (Cambridge, 1915).

with the dragon, but of his death and resurrection as it is found in his martyrdom at Cappodocia.

In this legend, George of Cappodocia comes forward against King Datianus, who has been persecuting the Christians of Persia. Datianus commands George to sacrifice to Apollo, but George blasphemes against all pagan deities. He is tortured and imprisoned. While in prison, God tells him he is to suffer seven years, and that he will be killed three times. At his fourth death he will enter paradise. All this comes to pass, and in the apocryphal version each of the tortures and deaths is rendered in the most explicit detail.[9]

At his first death, George is cut into ten pieces, but the Angel Michael collects all the pieces of the body. God touches them with His hand and revitalizes them. This kind of *sparagmos* places the figure of George directly in the tradition of Osiris, Dionysus, Orpheus, and Tammuz, all dying and reviving vegetation gods. This connection with the fertility spirit is further borne out by George's final death by decapitation when, instead of blood, milk and water flow from his body. The Hero-Combat, then, might be looked at as the dramatic expression of a form of religious consciousness distinct from those that appear to be reflected in the forms of the Wooing Ceremony and Sword Play. If we assume that this form is closest to monotheism, we might have one explanation of why a Christian figure like St. George was most easily assimilated into the structure of the Hero-Combat and why the Hero-Combat's popularity is so widespread and apparently durable. It is simply representative of a form of religion closest in quality of consciousness and religious belief to the Christian folk.

The Nature of the Ceremony Today

The English men's ceremonial lies somewhere between pure ritual and pure drama. The element of drama is clearly dominant as we know the ceremony today. The combatant who brandishes his sword and cries, "In comes I, St. George," is consciously imitating the hero-saint. The doctor who revives the corpse and then turns to the spectators, crying, "You can't get this on the National Health!" is clearly at a distance from the reality of his action. But the seasonal nature of the performance, the "bit of luck" that invests the appearance of the troupe with a vague sense of effective purpose, the need for anonymity as it is reflected in traditional costume, and the need for silence about the time and place of the troupe's appearance indicate traces of the original pure ritual from which the folk drama has emerged.

It is through these traces that we can still discern the origins of the individual types of ceremonies. Their basic underlying unity in the death and resurrection action can be explained by the fact that all find their source in a primitive rite of *plerosis.* The more confusing, disparate elements, on the other hand, may arise from the fact that each takes its dramatic structure from a distinctly different form of religious consciousness. The action of the Sword Play seems to originate in totemistic ritual while the central figure of the Wooing Ceremony seems the more individualized expression of the community, the fertility-*daimon.* In the Hero-Combat there appears the even more individualized protagonist of the legendary hero.

With the passage of time, however, the edges blur. Christianity replaces paganism in the religious consciousness. The church takes over the responsibility for the spiritual health of the community and the concept of the men's ceremonial as effective, magical, and necessary recedes. The people grow sophisticated and the procession and performance that once brought fertility to the land and the tribe become simply a luck-bringing perambulation. In the farms and fields it still retains traces of its ancient mysterious source. In the court it evolves into pure entertainment with the lyricism and splendor of the masque.[J] Communication grows between villages once virtually isolated from one another. The Sword Play takes on figures of the Hero-Combat. The Hero-Combat borrows action from the Wooing Ceremony. The Combat of the Wooing Ceremony gradually follows the shape of the Hero-Combat. A sense of nationalism grows along with religious consciousness and the mythic *daimons* and heroes melt into legendary historical figures and near-contemporary heroes. Industry replaces agriculture as the major support of the community. The factories do not look to the land and the change of the seasons to thrive. Whole communities fragment. Wars take away the men who perform the plays.

Today, in the last half of the twentieth century, the Sword Play is a breathtaking spectacle of rhythmic and acrobatic skill. The Hero-Combat

[J] For a full discussion of the relationship between the men's ceremonial and the masque, see Enid Welsford, *The Court Masque* (Cambridge, 1927).

is becoming a favorite schoolboy's exercise. The Wooing Play is vaguely remembered by some of the oldest inhabitants of the East Midlands. Every Christmas someone writes a sentimental letter to his newspaper, asking, "What has become of the dear old mummers' plays?" and some-one invariably answers that it is still performed in *his* village, at any rate. The answers will probably soon stop coming. Then the questions will disappear, too.

What is so extraordinary is that the process has taken so long; for it is almost a thousand years since there was any reason for the men of the town to meet on one night of the year, to hide their faces, to move from station to station through the town and, in the center of the magic circle, to re-enact the death and resurrection of their earth, the eternal pattern of the seasons.

APPENDICES, NOTES, INDEX

THE NETLEY ABBEY MUMMERS' PLAY

FIRST CHRISTMAS BOY

Ladies and Gentlemen, spectators all, I hope you are all
willing to hear the royal act, the royal act and our
treseter [*sic*] is yet but young.
We are all young hands we never act before,
We do the best we can, we cannot do no more.
So step in old Father Christmas from the door

(*Enter Father Christmas*)

In comes I, old Father Christmas
Welcome or welcome not,
I hope old Father Christmas
Will never be forgot.
Room, room, ladies and gentlemen, room I do obtain,
After me steps King George and all his noble train.
For in this room there shall soon a most dreadful
battle that ever was known
Betwixt King George and Turkey Snipe.
Enter in King George and boldly clear the way,
For old Father Christmas got a short time to stay.

(*Enter King George*)

In comes I, King George,

Reprinted from Alex Helm, *Five Mumming Plays for Schools* (London, 1965),
pp. 13–18.

King George that valiant man with courage bold,
'Twas I that won five crowns of gold.
'Twas I that fought the fiery dragon and brought him to a slaughter,
And by that fight I hope to win the Queen of Egypt's daughter.

TURKEY SNIPE

In comes I, Turkey Snipe,
Just come from Turkey Land old England for to fight.
I'll fight thee King Jarge that valent man,
That valent man of courage bold,
Let the blood be ever so hot
I'll shortly draw it cold.

KING GEORGE

Ah! ha! my little man
You talks brave and bold,
Just like some of these little lads I've been told.
Pull out your purse and pay.
Pull out your sword and fight.
Satisfaction I will have
Before I leave this night.

TURKEY SNIPE

No purse will I pull out,
No money will I pay,
But my sword I will draw out
And have satisfaction of thee this day.
Battle, battle, battle I will call,
And see which on the ground shall fall.

KING GEORGE

Battle, battle, I will cry,
To see which on the ground shall lie.
(*They fight. King George slays his opponent*)

KING GEORGE

Ladies and gentlemen all
Just see what miracles I have done.

I have cut thy father Abraham down
The like ever seen.
Pray! Pray! is there a doctor to be found
To cure this noble Turk lie bleeding on the ground.

(*Enter Doctor*)

Oh! yes! there is a doctor to be found
To cure this noble Turk lie bleeding on the ground.

KING GEORGE

What can you cure, doctor?

DOCTOR

I can cure all diseases;
I can cure the hitch, the stitch, the palsy and the gout,
Raging pain both inside and out.
If the devil's in a man, I'll fetch him out.
Give me an old woman four score and ten,
With scarcely a stump of a tooth in her head,
I will make her young and plump again.
More than this. If she falls downstairs and breaks her neck,
I will settle and charge nothing for my fees.
Recollect I am not like one of those bony back doctors
Who runs about from door to door telling a pack of lies,
I will shortly raise the dead before your eyes.

KING GEORGE

Where have you been learning all these fine things, doctor?

DOCTOR

I've been to England, Ireland, Scotland and Dover,
I have travelled the wide world over.

KING GEORGE

What is your fee, doctor?

DOCTOR

Ten guineas is my fee, thee being a poor man,
Half of that I'll take of thee.

KING GEORGE
>   Take that and cure him.

DOCTOR
>   I've a little bottle in the waistband of my trousers
>   Called the Oakham, smokum, altigam pain.
>   I drop one to his head, one to his heart,
>   Rise thou noble Turk, and take thy part.

TURKEY SNIPE
>   Now see, King George, I have rose again.
>   How long have I been on that horrid floor?
>   I've been hurried and scurried,
>   I have been dragged from door to door.
>   Is there a man can tell a task?
>   Pick me up a stranger,
>   Knock me down a blow,
>   Wherever I have been if the ground had not caught me
>   I do not know.

BEELZEBUB
>   In come I, little Tom Beelzebub,
>   On me 'ed I carries me nob,
>   In my 'and a drippin' pan-
>   Don't you think I'm a funny old man?

POOR AND MEAN
>   In comes I, Poor and Mean,
>   Hardly worthy to be seen.
>   Christmas comes but once a year,
>   When it comes it brings good cheer.
>   Roast beef, plum pudding, mince pie,
>   Who likes that any better and I? (*sic*)

GLUTTON
>   In comes I, Glutton,
>   I can eat roast beef, bacon, pork or mutton.
>   Although they call me poor and mean,
>   My old sword will cut fat or lean.

SCOTCH AND SCARS

> In comes I, Scotch and Scars,
> I've just come from those horrid wars.
> 'Twas he and I and seven more,
> Fought the battle of eleven score.
> Many a battle have I been in,
> Many a battle have I seen,
> Fighting for King George our king.

FAT AND FINE

> In comes I, Fat and Fine,
> Half starved, stone blind,
> Ricked back and broken mind,
> One eye out and t'other in,
> Don't you think I'm a funny old man?

JACK JOHN

> In comes I, little Jack John,
> If any man wants to fight, let him come on.
> I will hack him, I'll cut him,
> And after I'm done,
> I will fight the best man sits under the sun.
> My head is made of brass,
> Body lined with steel,
> Brass for my knuckle bones,
> I will fight you on the field.

SWEEP

> In comes I, Sweep,
> All I gets I keep.

TWING TWANG

> In comes I, Twing Twang
> I'm the lieutenant of all you press gang.
> I come to press all you bold mummers
> To send you to sea to fight the French,
> And drive the Russians right away.

If you had not like to believe what I have to say,
Step in Tipton Slasher and boldly clear the way.

TIPTON SLASHER

In comes I, Tipton Slasher,
Tipton Slasher is my name.
My broad sword spear buckled by my side
I am bound to win the game.

JOHNNY JACK

In comes I, little Johnny Jack,
With my wife and family at my back.
Although my wife is but small
I have to work hard to find bread and cheese for them all.
When I walk, I walk abroad;
When I sit, I sit at ease.
Ladies and Gentlemen, give the Christmas Boys what you please.
A jug of your Christmas ale will make us all merry and sing.
Money in my Christmas box is a very fine thing.

B

THE GREATHAM SWORD DANCE PLAY

Dancers: The King, Mr. Sparks, Mr. Stout, Mr. Wild, The Squire's Son, The Prince

Clowns: Rantom Tom, True Blue (Hector), The Doctor

RANTOM TOM

My master sent me here, some room for to provide,
So therefore gentle dears, stand back on every side,
For if he should come and find no room, he will bind me in his belt,
He will lay me down upon the ground and thrash me like a whelp,
He will make my bones like mice bones, like the ribs of little rats.
I once went a-courting to one Susie Perkins
Where the dogs and the cats made such a bow-wowing and barking
    I forgot what to say.
What the dickens must I say?
Gurn before your nose and see before your eyes,
And if you don't mind, some of these bonny lads will take you by
    surprise.
(*Sings to 1st tune*)
They sent me before to knock at your door
To see if you'd let us come in.
Although I'm a clown they call me a fool,

Reprinted from Norman Peacock, "The Greatham Sword Dance," *JEFDSS*, VIII (December, 1956), 29–39.

To please our gallant fine king.
Although I am little I'm made of good metal
I'll scorn for to tell you a lie:
I once killed an urchin as big as myself,
Which made me both lamb and goose pie.
My coat is made of stand-off, stand-off,
My trousers are made of mohair,
My stockings and shoes, they are made of refuse,
And my sword is "Come strike if you dare."
(He strikes at the air with his sword)

MR. STOUT
(sings to 2nd tune)
Our King he will come in, dressed in his grandarie,
He'll call his young men in by one by two by three.

KING
(walks round in a counter-clockwise circle and sings to 2nd tune)
Now the first is Mr. Sparks, he's lately come from France;
He's the first man on our list and the second in our dance.

MR. SPARKS
(follows King and sings)
God bless your honoured fame and all your young men too:
I've come to act my part as well as I can do.

KING
The next is Mr. Stout, as I do understand,
As good a swordsman he, as ever took sword in hand.

MR. STOUT
(following Mr. Sparks)
I often have been tried in city, town and field,
I never could meet the man that ever could make me yield.

KING
The next that I call on, he is a squire's son;
I'm afraid he'll lose his love because he is too young.

SQUIRE'S SON

(*following Mr. Wild*)

Although I be too young, I have money for to roam,
I'll freely spend it all before I'll lose my love.

KING

The last he is a prince, he is born of noble fame;
He spent a large estate the wars for to maintain.

PRINCE

(*following Squire's Son*)

Although I be the last, my name I'll not deny,
Although I be the last, my valour here I'll try,
And I'll not daunted be, although I be the last,
For I can act my part as well as all the rest.

1ST CLOWN

Nay but I'm the last mesel, my name is Rantom Tom,
and the lasses you've got here I'll kiss them every one.

2ND CLOWN

Gadzooks I clean forgot that I was one of your crew,
If you want to know my name, my name it is True Blue.

ALL

We are six dancers bold, as bold as you can see.
We have come to dance this dance to please the company.
Our dancers are but young, and seldom danced before,
We will do the best we can, the best can do no more.
It's not for greedy gain this ramble we do take,
But what you please to give our clowns will freely take.
You've seen us all go round, so think of us what you will;
Music strike up and play, we're the lads from Greatham still.

1ST DANCE

2ND CLOWN

Here comes I that never come yit,
With my big head and my little wit:

Although my head be big and my wit be small,
I can act my part as well as you all.
So room! Room! my brave gallants (*swings his sword round*)
   Listen what I've got to say.
My name is bold Hector and I'll clear the way;
Hector, Hector, the banberry bush, me mother's sister's son-in-law.
There's great Tom Paynes standing staring, swearing at the door
And he winnat come in, he's a poor silly fool like thee (*to King*)
He'll swear more over one inch of candle than thou wouldst over a
   ten-pound note burning away.
   (*to King*)   Harks thee my canny man, listen what I've got to say,
      Wasn't that thou stealing swine the other day?

KING

   Stealing what?

2ND CLOWN

   Feeding swine, I meant to say.

KING

   Come young men and try your rapiers on this villain, or he'll stand
      prating to me all day.
   (*to Clown*) We're going to try you for sheep stealing.
   (*The dancers then make the Lock about the Clown loosely,*
   each man turning clockwise on the spot and standing with
   hilt crossed over point.)

2ND CLOWN

   Will you give me time to make my will and say my prayers?
   (*The dancers assent*)
   My son Basto I'll leave thee my old spotted cow, and see that thou
      takes good care of her.

ALL

   So I will Dad!

2ND CLOWN

   My son Taylor, I'll leave thee my lapp-board and shears, and see
      that thou makes good use of them.

ALL

So will I Dad!

2ND CLOWN

My son Fiddler, I'll leave thee my backbone for fiddlestick, small
bones for fiddle-strings.

(*to King*) And as for thou, I'll leave thee the ringbone of my eye
for a Jack-whistle.

So ladies and gentlemen all, I bid you all farewell.

(*The dancers tighten up the Lock around the Clown's neck
and then draw their swords and the Clown falls down dead.*)

KING

A doctor! A doctor! Ten pounds for a doctor!

DOCTOR

(*enters*)

Here am I, what is thy will with me?

KING

Here's a man fallen upstairs and broken his neck.

DOCTOR

Fallen upstairs and broken his neck! I never heard tell of such a
thing.

KING

Downstairs I mean, Doctor; thou's so full of thee catches.

Where dost thou live, Doctor?

DOCTOR

I live in Itty-titty, where there's neither town nor city,

Wooden churches with black puddings for bell-ropes;

Little dogs and cats running about with knives and forks stuck in
their paws, shouting, "God Save the Queen."

KING

How far dost thou travel, Doctor?

DOCTOR

From the fireside to the bedside.

KING

What, and no further?

DOCTOR

Yes, the cheese-and-bread cupboard.

KING

I thought thou was a cheese-and-bread eater.
What is thy fee, Doctor?

DOCTOR

My fee is, 19 19s 11-3/4 d, but 19 19s 1-3/4 s I'll take from thee.

KING

Well! Set to work Doctor and I'll see thee paid or unpaid in the
morning.

DOCTOR

That will never do for me—"A bird in the hand is worth two in
the bush," so I'll go home, indeed that I will.

KING

Nay! Nay! Stay Doctor and I'll see thee paid out of my own pocket.

DOCTOR

How long has this man been dead?

KING

Just half-an-hour since we took off his head.

DOCTOR

It's a long time for a man to be dead and brought alive again, but
however I'll try my skill.
(*Examines Clown*)
Here's a leg broken and an arm broken and his wind-cutter's loose.

No matter ladies and gentlemen, I am a doctor who travels far
and near and much at home;

Take these my pills to cure all ills—the past, the present and to
come.

The gout, the itch, the sores, the stitch, the money-grubs and the
burley-stubs,

All out of this little dandarious box of mine;

Thousands have I erracted and as many more distracted.

Now is there any young man in this company got a scolding wife?

Bring her to me in the morning and I'll give her one pill of the sivil
that'll send her headlong to the divil.

So I'm a doctor that can cure all aches, pains, cramps and sprains,

And take away all wrinkles, hiccough, headache, backache, bellyache,
toothache and migrains.

I'll make the paper smock to crack, and soon remove the pain of
love and cure the love-sick maid,

The young, the old, the hot, the cold, the living and the dead.

I can make the deaf to hear, the dumb to speak, the lame to walk
and fly.

KING

Dame Doctor, you lie!

DOCTOR

How can I lie when I'm walking on this ground?—I'm better than
any doctor.

I can cure any pretty maid that goes bow-legged, old bones, strange
in back;

Big stout maids and whisky-jades.

I can make any person or persons fly over nine iron hedges,

Such as old Kate Rickerburn, the mother of fifteen dead, born alive;

Two misfortunes in one night; broke a pot, cut her arm,

And besides that the old lady could crack a marble.

Now is there any young women in this company would like a little
of my ink-a-tink, white drops of life? (*Produces a bottle*)

Look here, when I was late in Asia, I gave two spoonfuls to the
great Megull, my grandmother,

Which caused her to have two boys and three girls.

She was then the age of ninety-nine, and she swore if she lived nine
hundred years longer, she would never be without two spoonfuls
of this excellent cordial of mine for a safe deliverance on a cold
and frosty morning.
Two spoonfuls will cure the cuckle and take away its horns.
So my cork I'll pull out, my business to complete:
Soon you will see this young man stand up on his feet.
(*Gives the Clown a drink*)
I'll scour him over and over again. (*Does so*)
Judge and try, if he die, never believe me more,
But if I find his spirits fail,
I'll blow him up as if the devil was in his tail.

CLOWN

(*Rises and sings to 2nd tune*)
Good morrow gentlemen, a-sleeping I have been;
I have had such a sleep as the likes was never seen;
But now I am awake and alive unto this day,
And now we'll have a dance, and the Doctor must seek his pay.

2ND DANCE

C

THE BASSINGHAM MEN'S PLAY 1823 XMAS

(*Enter Fool*)
> Good Evening Ladys and Gentlemen all
> This merry time at Christmas I have made it bold to call
> I hope you will not take it ill what I am a going to say
> I have some more Boys & Girls drawing on this way
> I have some little Boys stands at the Door
> In Ribbons they are neatly dressed
> For to please you all they shall do their best
>   Step in Merrymen all.

(*The players enter and sing together*)
> Good Master and good Mistress
>   As you sit by the Fire
> Remember us poor Ploughlads
>   That runs through Mud and Mire
>
> The mire it is deep
>   And we travel far and near
> We will thank you for a Christmas Box
>   And a mug of your strong Beer.

FOOL
> Bastard you Jade its none of mine
> Its not a bit like me

Reprinted from Charles Read Baskerville, "Mummers' Wooing Plays in England," *MP*, XXI (February 1924), 241–245, used with the permission of the University of Chicago Press.

I am a Valient Hero lately Come from Sea
You never see me before, now did you
I slew Ten men with a Seed of Mustard
Ten thousand with an old Crush'd Toad
What do you think to that Jane
If you don't be of [f] I serve you the same.

OLD MAN

Here comes the poor old ancient Man
I speak for myself the best I can
My old grey Hairs they Hang so low
I do the best for myself the best I know.
(*To Lady*)
Me thinks me sees that star shine bright
On you Iv fix'd my hearts delight

In comes the Lady

Away Away from me be gone
Do you think I Marry such a Drone
No I have one of high degree
And not such an helpless wretch as the

OLD MAN

Kick me Lady out of the room
I be hang over our Kitchen Door

ST. GEORGE

In comes Saint George
    The Champeon bold
With my blooddy spear
    I have won Ten Thousand pounds in Gold
I fought the finest Dragon
    And brought him to a slaughter
And by that means I gaind
    The King of Egypts Daughter
I ash him and smash him as small as Flys
Send him to Jamaica to make Minch pies.

FOOL

    You hash me and smash me as small as flys
    Send me to Jamaica to make Minch Pies

The finishing Song

FOOL

    Come write me down the power above
    That first created A man to Love
    I have a Diamond in my eye
    Where all my Joy and comfort ly

    I give you Gold I give you Pearl
    If you can Fancy me my Girl
    Rich Costley Robes you shall wear
    If you can Fancy me my Dear

LADY

    Its not your Gold shall me entice
    Leave of [f] Virtue to follow your advice
    I do never intend at all
    not to be at any Young Mans call

FOOL

    Go you away you Proud and scornful Dame
    If you had been true I should of been the same
    I make no dought but I can find
    As handsome a fair one too my mind

LADY

    O stay Young Man you seem in haste
    Or are you afraid your time should waste
    Let reson rule your roving mind
    And perhaps in time she'l proof more kind

FOOL

    Now all my sorrows is comd and past
    Joy and comfort I have found at last
    The Girl that use to say me nay
    She comforts me both Night & Day.

D

EXCURSUS ON THE ENTERTAINMENT AT REVESBY

It has probably been noted that we have studiously avoided using the *Revesby Play* in our discussion of the English men's ceremonial. This is because there is still serious doubt as to the play's authenticity as a pure folk piece. The *Revesby Play* is a most curious phenomenon. In every survey of the *genre,* mention is sure to be made of the play, and that mention is apt to be peculiarly evasive. It is always a "strange" play, [1] or faintly "literary," [2] or simply "transitional." [3] When T. F. Ordish first published it, he noted all the disparate elements of various types of folk play from which it drew. He pointed out the allusions to Christmas which would ordinarily link it with the Hero-Combat; the Sword Dance; the use of the hobby-horse; the identification of the actors as plough-boys, yet the absence of the fool plough. He noted the entirely unfamiliar names assigned to the fool's sons and the "female," and then, to complicate matters further, published it under the title of *"Morrice Dancers* at Revesby."

The play was performed in Revesby Abbey, Lincolnshire, on October 20, 1779; neither Christmas, the traditional time for the Mummers' Plays nor Plough Monday, the time for the Wooing Ceremony. Ordish makes an attempt to explain this as a holdover of the Roman custom of a sword dance on October 19 in the celebration called the *Armilustrium,* but he throws it out only as a conjecture and offers no real support of the theory beyond the proximity of dates. Violet Alford suggests that it has some direct connection with Rent Day, especially since it ends with the Song of the Landlord and Tennant. [4] But Ordish points out that although this connects with the date of the whole performance, it only emphasizes the disparity with the direct allusions to the Christmas season present in the play. I believe Miss Alford's theory to be closer to the correct one.

In addition to these baffling elements, there is a definite literary strain which Chambers notes in the "comparative freedom from verbal and metrical irregularities." [5] This idea becomes even stronger with the theory that the naturalist, Sir Joseph Banks, was "responsible" for the play in some way.[A]

Much of the difficulty critics and scholars have had in dealing with the *Revesby Play* rises, I believe, from the fact that it is always considered in terms of pure folk drama. If, however, it is recognized as a much more sophisticated type of entertainment, consciously drawing on the elements of folk drama with which its audience was familiar rather than a pure, orally transmitted folk piece, many of the irregularities of structure and language can be resolved.

The *Revesby Play* takes its basic structure from none of the three types of English ceremonial. For a while it looks as if it may be a highly elaborate Hero-Combat, but then, a few lines later in the text, we are watching a Sword Dance and then, later still, we find ourselves in the middle of the Fool's Wooing. When Adams published it as an example of folk drama,[B] he claimed that it was actually a series of three plays which the plough-boys had, "in their enthusiasm," combined, with the first play ending on line 65, the second on line 258 and the last on line 569. He does not consider the Song of the Landlord and Tenant as part of the entertainment, although according to John Brand and Ordish it immediately followed the dance after line 569.[6]

In my reading of the play I have found eight distinct sections which, along with the Song of the Landlord and Tenant, has led me to consider the play similar to a modern revue in which various elements are strung together with only a minimal connection beyond the audience's recognition of the separate parts as familiar folk pieces.

[A] M. W. Barley, "Plough Plays in the East Midlands," *JEFDSS,* VII (1952), 70. Barley never specifies whether he believes Banks's contribution was as a writer or producer. When Miss Alford supports this theory, she goes so far as to say she believes Banks wrote it.

[B] Joseph Quincy Adams, *Chief Pre-Shakespearean Dramas* (Cambridge, 1924), pp. 357–364. All line citations are from Adams.

The first part of the play runs to line 28. It is the Fool's presentation, not of the first play which Adams would call "The Morris Dance of the Hobby Horse," but of the entire entertainment. It is being played for a single, mixed audience of the "gentle lords of honor, of high and low," (1–2) rather than moving from house to house. In lines 17–22 we can see a consciousness of the different forms at work.

> We are come over the mire and moss;
> We dance an Hobby Horse;
> A dragon you shall see,
> And a Wild Worm for to flee.
>> Still we are all brave jovial boys,
>> And take delight in Christmas toys.

With "mire and moss" the connection is immediately made with the Plough Play. The idea that the players take "delight in Christmas toys," does not necessarily mean, here, a specific Christmas *quête,* which would tell us that this is to be a traditional Hero-Combat Play out of season. It could simply allude to the delight of the performers in playing, just like the tradition of playing at Christmas. It is mumming itself that is the "Christmas toy." [c]

Part II is simply the song, "I Love to Have Money in Both Pockets," introduced after a short dialogue between the Fool and the Fiddler. Although this is not set off by itself in the text, it is clear from the way the play is recorded that time was taken for the song before the next part of the entertainment began. It is introduced with something like a modern song cue. The Fool says, "Ah! boy, times is hard! I love to have money in both pockets." (It should be noted that the quotation marks which Adams prints around he song title are not present in the original version of the play reproduced by Ordish.)

> Fiddler: You shall have it, old father.
> Fool: Let me see it. (32–35)

It is presumably here that the song was sung, for the direction immediately following the last line reads, "The Fool *then* calls in his five sons" [Italic mine].

---

[c] The O.E.D. gives the following use of the word "toys" as late as 1777: "A sportive or frisky movement; a piece of fun, amusement or entertainment; a fantastic or trifling speech or piece of writing."

The subsequent dance of the Fool and his five Sons constitutes Part III of the entertainment, running to line 66. It appears to be a dance performed by all six players. The Fool first calls in his five sons, Pickle Herring, Blue Britches, Ginger Britches, Pepper Britches and Mr. Allspice. All six "foot it once round the room" and then, while the first verse of the song is being sung, one performer exits and returns at the end of the verse riding the hobby-horse. The fight between the fool and the hobby-horse on the sidelines while the focus is on the singers and dancers is a familiar feature of the morris.

There has been a great deal of conjecture about Wild Worm, which is "sprung three or four times" during the song, and the Dragon which is called on immediately afterward. Adams believes they are the same thing, but since a distinction between them is explicitly made both in this section and in the promise of the Presentation, there must have been two devices. They would have worked something like this: after the first verse, the hobby-horse would make its appearance and the interest of the spectators would be on the fight between the Fool and the hobby-horse during the second verse. At the end of the second verse, the "Wild Worm," some kind of mechanical spectacle device, would be exhibited while a morris step was being executed by the sons. The man operating the Wild Worm would then exit, and during the third verse, "Come in, come in, thou Dragon stout," attention would go back to the Fool and the hobby-horse. Between the third and the fourth verses, the Dragon, a second spectacular device, would be presented in the same manner as the Wild Worm. This could explain the curious direction of the text that the "Wild Worm is *only sprung* [italics mine] three or four times." It would allow the operator of the Wild Worm to get off and return again with the Dragon device as well as avoid completely satisfying the audience's delight when there was another, similar device yet to come. At the fourth verse, "Now you shall see a full fair fight / Between our old fool and his right," the attention would return the Fool and hobby-horse, continuing through "Now our scrimmage is almost done." After the fifth verse, the hobby-horse is vanquished and exits, which accounts for the Fool's singing alone with "Up well hart, and up well hind." The end of the sequence is marked by a verse in the same metre as the end of the Presentation spoken or sung by the Fool alone, again with the "Christmas toys" allusion, another morris step around the room and a general exit. The exit also serves the purpose of allowing the dancers to get their swords and return for Part IV.

With Part IV, lines 67 to 258, we have a full-fledged Sword Play, performed by five dancers. The stage direction reads simply, "They all re-enter and lock their swords to make the glass." But this must have been preceded by at least a preliminary circle of the traditional Sword Dance if not more elaborate figures. Once the Lock is made, obviously in the form of a pentagon, it is used as the "glass" which leads to the comic sketch between Pickle Herring and the Fool. The first part of this section climaxes with the Fool flinging the lock down and stamping on it, a signal to break the lock. The lock is made three more times during the course of the dance, each time, now, as a part of the decapitation of the Fool. Each time the cure is signalled by Pickle Herring stamping his foot. In the original version, counter to Adam's edition, the entire section; including the Fool's will, is in prose until line 239 which begins the final decapita- tion and resurrection. The last figure of the Sword Dance is signaled by the Fool's line, "But I will rise, your sport then to advance, and with you all, brave boys, I'll have a dance." (256–8)

There are also a number of echoes of the Hero-Combat in the speeches of this section including such topsy-turvy images as,

> As I was a-looking round about me through my wooden specta- cles made of a great, huge, little, tiney, bit of leather, placed right behind me, even before me . . . (70–73)

and nonsense speeches. It is during one of these nonsense speeches that a new allusion to Christmas is made which has disturbed most commenta- tors on the play. If the allusion is considered in the context of the speech, however, I do not see the difficulty. It is worth quoting in full here, since it appears to be so troublesome.

> Now, gentlemen, you see how ungrateful my children is grown! When I had them at home, small, about as big as I am, I put them out to good learning: I put them to Coxcomb College, and then to the University of Loggerheads; *and I took them home again this good time of Christmas,* and I examined them all one by one, all together for shortness . . . (172–181)

There is nothing else in the speech which has any bearing on a reality outside the context of the antics of the Fool and his Sons and I do not see why this simple allusion should be an exception. Indeed, if my reading of the reference to Christmas in the Presentation is correct, then this is simply another allusion to what a *Christmas-like* entertainment this is.

Chambers also sees several echoes of the Hero-Combat tradition in the song at the end of the dance.[7] But the variations in the traditional lines are so sophisticated here, they only help to confirm the idea that there was a conscious mind at work in assembling the *Revesby Play.* For instance, the traditional line of St. George reads something like this:

> My head is made of cannon balls
> My body's made of steel,
> My arms and legs of the first class brass.

In the *Revesby Play,* the Sons, with their swords locked around the Fool's neck, say:

> Our old Fool's bracelet is not made
> of gold,
> But it is made of iron and good steel,
> And unto death we'll make this old fool
> yield. (238–242)

Later, when the Fool rushes in, after having been onstage almost consistently since the Presentations, the traditional line most often assigned to Little Jack Doubt,

> Here come I that never been yit,
> With my big head and little wit . . .

becomes

> Here comes I that never come yet,
> Since last time, lovey!
> I have a great head but little wit. (293)

I cannot believe that the broken rhythm of "Since last time, lovey!" is not a conscious comic stroke depending on the audience's unquestionable familiarity with the traditional words.

Sections v and vi are both short interludes, the first a dance called *Jack the Brisk Young Drummer,* danced by Cicely and the Foreman while the other performers remain onstage, and the second a short caper by the Fool while the five sword dancers change costume.

The Fool's "Sound, music! I must be gone; the Lord of Pool draws nigh," (263–5) introduces Section VII, a second complete Sword Dance, this time with each dancer singing his own verse of the traditional Calling-on-Song and culminating in Nelly's Gig and a series of flashy figures described in the directions.

The final section of the play, as presented by Adams, draws directly on the Plough Play for the Fool's Wooing. Although interspersed with Morris Dances, it is clearly a unit from line 239–569. As noted before, there are many more variations on the wooing action than in most versions of the Wooing Ceremony, but the basis is there. Another indication that this is an entirely new section comes with the new roles the dancers take, with Pickle Herring now as the old man and the Fool as the young Noble Anthony. This Plough Play is the climactic part of the entertainment. Not only do all the performers take part in it, but elements of all three types of folk play that have appeared up to now blend into one another and contribute to the action. The Fool's lines from 298 to 303 constitute what could be considered an entirely new presentation with the call for room and particularly the use of the curious word "activity" in line 200. In line 367, the actor still designated as Blue Britches calls "Strike up the Morris Dance!" and proceeds to "foot it once round" with Cicely. Each of the performers reintroduces himself with a new set of Sword Dance verses. And the whole is structured on the Wooing Ceremony action. There are numerous other echoes of traditional speeches such as "thy face shines like a dripping pan," (443) and "thy nose stands like a Maypole tree," (552) which connect one kind of folk entertainment with another in a thoroughly ingenious manner.

At the end of Section VIII, the Song of the Landlord and the Tenant was sung by two men who had accompanied the players but had not taken part in the performance. This is the *Revesby Play's* conscious, ironic twist on the *quête* of the traditional play. Besides the message of the song, ". . . you Tennants must obey, And pay the Landlords their rents twice a year," two other circumstances support the idea here of a *quête*. The traditional *quête* of the men's ceremonial generally occurs after the main entertainment with the introduction of new players to make the collection. This, of course, is exactly what occurs in the *Revesby Play,* except that here the *quête* is being made on October 20, for the rent of the tenants rather than donations.

It is claimed that the text of the *Revesby Play* is the oldest extant example of folk drama. However, I do not believe we can accept it as pure folk literature. Whether or not Sir Joseph Banks actually wrote it, the idea is inescapable that there was a single, controlling hand involved, and that that hand was familiar enough with all the types of folk play to manipulate and arrange them into an entertainment very different from the spontaneous, traditional play peculiar to a particular festival, but able to draw on all of them for the delight of an audience whose recognition of those forms was taken for granted.

E

EXCURSUS ON THE PAPA STOUR TEXT

The element of literary interference in the development of the men's ceremonial is at its clearest in the Papa Stour text. We have only to look at the Epilogue to this version of the Sword Play to be struck by a kind of self-consciousness and literary imagery we have encountered nowhere else in this examination.

> Mars does rule, he bends his brows
> He makes us all agast; [*sic*]
> After the few hours that we stay here,
> Venus will rule at last.
> Farewell, farewell, brave gentles all,
> That herein do remain,
> I wish you health and happiness
> Till we return again.[1]

Allusion to classical mythic figures, diction like "agast," imagery like Mars "bending his brows" are clear indications that a literary tone, outside the natural flow of tradition, has been imposed. It is also in evidence throughout the text as we have it.

Strangely enough, however, Papa Stour is one of the earliest documents in the whole field of folk collection. Chambers, in his reproduction of the text, includes some interesting material to help establish the early dating of the text. He gives us, first of all, an entry in Sir Walter Scott's diary for August 7, 1814, in which he tells of an account of the Papa Stour sword dance. "There are eight performers," Scott says,

156

seven of whom represent the Seven Champions of Christendom, who
enter one by one with their swords drawn, and are presented to the
eighth personage, who is not named. Some rude couplets are spoken
(in *English* not Norse) containing a sort of panegyric upon each
champion as he is presented. They then dance a sort of cotillion, as the
ladies described it, going through a number of evolutions with their
swords. One of my three Mrs. Scotts readily promised to procure me
the lines, the rhyme and the form of the dance. . . . In a stall pamphlet,
called the history of Buckhaven, (Fifeshire), it is said those fishers
sprung from Danes, and brought with them their *war-dance* or *sword
dance,* and a rude wooden cut of it is given.[2]

Chambers then gives us the text of Papa Stour as it appeared in a note to
Scott's *The Pirate,* 1821. In this note, Scott characterizes the dance as "a
species of play or mystery, in which the seven champions of Christendom
make their appearance as in the interlude presented in *All's Well that
Ends Well."* [3] Then follows the text itself and a final note stating that
the manuscript from which the text was copied is known "from various
circumstances," to have been written by William Henderson about 1788.
Henderson's manuscript itself is claimed to have been transcribed from
"a very old one." [4]

There is an odd disparity, however, between the description Scott records in his 1814 diary account and the text he reproduces in 1821. The
1821 text gives us the Master, in the form of St. George, introducing
James of Spain, Dennis of France, David of Wales, Patrick of Ireland,
Anthony of Italy, and Andrew of Scotland. This makes seven performers,
including the Master, not the eight of Scott's diary. And the six who follow the Master are clearly being introduced to the spectators, "brave
gentles all," not an "unnamed eighth personage."

In addition to this, the words with which the champions are introduced
are neither "rude" as they are characterized in the Diary account, nor are
they in couplet form. We have already seen examples of the rude couplets
that introduce the dancers in the Calling-on Songs of Greatham, Bellerby,
and Earsdon. The difference in the level of verbal and technical sophistication between Greatham's calling-on verses and the Papa Stour Master's
song are apparent even at first glance. Here is Greatham:

> KING
> Now the first is Mr. Sparks, he's lately
>   come from France;

He's the first man on our list and the
second in our dance.

MR. SPARKS

God bless your honoured fame and all your
young men too:
I've come to act my part as well as I can
do.

KING

The next is Mr. Stout, as I do understand,
As good a swordsman he, as ever took sword
in hand.

MR. STOUT

I often have been tried in city, town and
field,
I never could meet the man that ever could
make me yield.[5]

These lines, with their monotonous rhythm, simple sentence structure and
aa, bb, cc, dd rhyme scheme can, indeed, be called, "rude."

Now let us look at similar introductory verses from Scott's Papa Stour
text:

Brave Champion Dennis, a French knight,
Who stout and bold is to be seen,
Present thyself here in our sight,
Thou brave French knight,
Who bold hast been;
Since thou such valiant acts hast done,
Come let us see some of them now
With courtesy, thou brave French knight,
Draw out thy sword of noble hue.

(*Dennis dances while the others
retire to a side.*)

Brave David a bow must string, a with awe
Set up a wand upon a stand,
And that brave David will cleave in twa.

(*David dances solus*) [6]

The rhyme scheme, alternation of stress and control of changes in line feet here are far from "rude."

Of further interest is the sense of the pyrrhic nature of the ceremony that emerges from the Papa Stour text. All through the Master's song, the ideas of chivalric valour, bravery and exploits of the sword are stressed. When he introduces Andrew of Scotland, for instance, the Master sings:

> Thou kindly Scotsman, come thou here;
> Thy name is Andrew of Fair Scotland;
> Draw out they sword that is most clear,
> Fight for thy king with thy right hand;
> And aye as long as thou canst stand,
> Fight for thy king with all thy heart.[7]

Anthony of Italy's verses run:

> Draw out thy sword that is most clear,
> And do thou fight without any doubt;
> Thy leg thou shake, thy neck thou lout,
> And show some courtesy on this floor,
> For we shall have another bout,
> Before we pass out of this boor.[8]

Thus far, except in the modern version of Earsdon, this identification of the dancers as fighting champions has not had much relevance. In the three versions we have examined in the body of this study, the members of the troupe were characterized as travelers, suitors and workers. Furthermore, the purpose of the dance in all the other versions was collection and celebration. In Papa Stour the Master implies a very different motive for the dance when he urges the champions to "prove their manhood" on the floor and, after his first introduction of the company, sings,

> . . . Let us come to sport,
> Since that ye have a mind to war.
> Since that ye have this bargain sought,
> Come let us fight and do not fear.[9]

It will be noticed that the 1814 diary description, given to Scott by the ladies, contains no pyrrhic connotations of this sort at all. It is, in fact, described as a sort of "cotillion." It is only the pamphlet to which he later alludes that characterizes the ceremony as Danish in origin and a *"war dance."* There is certainly nothing pyrrhic about the complete dance as described in the 1821 text. Once the circle of dancers is formed, the swords serve no combat-like purpose. They are merely dealt with as links, held hilt and point. These links are never broken during the course of the dance, except for the formation of the lock, and even in that figure there is no pyrrhic movement involved.[A]

If, then, Scott's diary account of the Papa Stour ceremony is a reliable one of a true folk ritual, we cannot conclude that the 1821 text in *The Pirate* is a record of the ceremony described in that account. It is, rather, a curious mixture of folk ceremony and imposed literary explanations. It seems likely that the "Words" of the Papa Stour text as we have them from William Henderson's version were literary creations.

If this is true, we can then account for the disparity between the eye-witness account and the text. Even after the accretion of the new literary Calling-on Song, the ceremony must have continued in its natural flow of development. The "Words," preserved in manuscript, continued to be handed down orally by the dancers until they evolved into the "rude couplets" heard by Mrs. Scott, while Henderson, in going to "the very old manuscript," reproduced the original verses which had remained uncorrupted by the oral tradition.

The Papa Stour Ceremony contains the Calling-on Song, the circle of linked dancers and the formation of the Lock as features in common with other sword ceremonies. It lacks the death, the resurrection, the accompanying clowns and we can infer no mimetic action at all from the text. All of this can be attributed to the clear literary interference which we have traced.

Papa Stour is valuable in any study of the men's ceremonial, for it appears to be an early example of a late stage of development. It is a literary document guiding us to the action of an already highly representa-

[A] The very title Scott gives his record of the text suggests this kind of literary rationalization of the dance. It is called, "Words used as a Prelude to the Sword Dance, a Danish or Norwegian Ballet, composed some centuries ago, and preserved in Papa Stour, Zetland." *Ibid.,* p. 272. There is an ambiguity here about whether the phrase "composed some centuries ago" refers to the ballet or words. In either case the suggestion of the application of a conscious, creative hand cannot be avoided. Nor can we avoid the sense of the words and the dance as separate entities rather than related elements of a unified action.

tional and selective version. The repetition of solo performances demonstrates the emphasis of artistic achievement and the nature of the words indicates that literary self-consciousness has already firmly established itself, while the linked dance, with its formation of the lock, points to its original nature as a ritual.

F

LINES 109–131 OF *THE ALCESTIS*

LEADER: To wander o'er leagues of land
　　　To search over wastes of sea,
　　Where the prophets of Lycia stand,
　　　Or where Ammon's daughters three
　　Make runes in the rainless sand,
　　　For magic to make her free
　　　　　Ah, vain! For the end is here;
　　　　　Sudden it comes and sheer.
　　What lamb on the altar-strand
　　　Stricken shall comfort me?

SECOND ELDER: Only, only one, I know:
　　　Apollo's son was he,
　　Who healed men long ago.
　　　Were he but on earth to see,
　　She would rise from the dark below
　　　And the gates of eternity
　　　　　For men Gods had slain
　　　　　He pitied and raised again;
　　Till God's fire laid him low,
　　And now what help have we?

Reprinted from Euripides, *The Alcestis,* tr. Gilbert Murray (New York, 1936), lines 109–131, with the permission of Oxford University Press.

162

G

THE RUMANIAN KALUSARI PLAY

*The following is an extract from Alex Helm's manuscript of his Lectures
at Keele University, Folk Studies Conference, Keele University (Summer
1966), pp. 166–171. It constitutes a most complete summary of the
filmed action of the Kalusari or Little Horse Dancers of Rumania and
Slobozia and a New Year's Dance from Bukovina. The film was made c.
1935 and is a part of the Vaughan Williams Library Collection, Cecil
Sharp House, London.*

By extreme good fortune a performance of the primitive action was
recorded on film by a chance visitor: the film, or at any rate portions of it,
we are going to see. The film shows how much of the action is expressed
in simple dance, and how much the costume, maintaining the disguise,
has persisted. The mute has a mask made from the skin of a freshly
flayed goat worn bloody side out, with the tail forming the beard, and the
hats of the dancers are, as is usual, splendidly decorated.

The action of the ceremony can be summarised as follows. Four men
holding their poles horizontally between each other, form a square to
represent a castle, and dance, or shuffle their feet, throughout the whole
action. This particular performance is given by two teams and there are
consequently two mutes, one of whom brings a cloth and hangs it on one
of the poles to represent a window. The mute then takes possession of the
castle and brings a chair and a piece of sacking for a carpet, to furnish
it. There is by-play between the mutes as each tries to claim the castle
by fighting for it. One mute begins to kill lice with his wooden phallus,
the other meanwhile tries to saw the first mute's head off using his wooden

163

phallus as a sword. One mute takes his shirt off to de-louse it. Next comes a procession led by the Turkish overlord, wearing a white dress, a wide red cummerbund and fez. He is smoking a bullrush soaked in paraffin to represent a pipe, and carries a whip. To let him enter the castle one of the men forming the walls lets go his stick which opens like a door, but the mutes have to go through the walls. The overlord is thus in possession of his castle, from which he runs out from time to time, to lash the crowd with his whip and collect dues and tribute. The mutes take his absences as an opportunity to return, but they leave as soon as he re-enters. Finally, the Turk assumes occupation of the castle and looks for a bride.

She enters in procession, veiled and accompanied by the mutes, bringing with her her distaff for spinning, and she spins all the time. The Turk registers matrimonial conditions, and from time to time leaves the castle to collect his tribute. Whilst he is away from the castle the mutes re-enter and torment the wife. Ultimately the Turk and his wife are shown to be an old settled married couple, who are seen to go for a walk in the garden of their home. This walk takes the form of a gentle dance movement.

Then enters the Russian, shown to be an obnoxious character, dressed in red rags roughly bound round him, spitting vodka from a bottle and splashing the liquor over the watching crowd. He also carries a whip. Behind him is a priest of the Orthodox Church, riding in a wheelbarrow, dragging his begging box behind. The Russian enters the castle and attacks the wife, being discovered doing so by the Turk. The fight which follows is carried out by their lashing each other with whips, and is repeated several times. The Russian is so drunk by this time that he does not understand what is happening when the Turk singes his nose with the hot pipe, and he makes continuous attacks. By this time, the wife has become complacent to the Russian's advances, and the Turk has lost interest in her. The Russian dances with her and forces vodka down her throat, and ultimately, the priest enters and attacks her. The Turk seeks revenge for this and drives the priest all round the compound, holding him by the begging box and beating him with the whip. The Russian rescues the priest who hobbles off and climbs a nearby roof where in pantomime, he acts God the Father giving Moses the Commandments.

Whilst the priest is on the roof, a shot is fired, and the Turk is killed. The wife arranges the body and mourns over it, the Russian goes over to the Priest and tells him to bury the Turk, but the Priest refuses. The Russian now triumphant, spills more vodka over the wife still mourning over the body, whose face she covers with a cloth. She is again insulted by the mutes. The priest is brought in in his wheelbarrow, but first refuses to conduct the funeral: later he carries out a perfunctory Christian burial service over the infidel Turk. The Russian insults the widow and finally, in the last details of the burial, sits on his victim's head. The body is then raised by the men who formed the walls and is borne away, followed by the villagers. There is no revival.

The next scene shows the Calusari from Slobozia preparing their standard by binding on the garlic and kerchief to the pole. The Captain does the binding whilst the members of the team hold the post, which is raised and brought forward. The mute puts his symbol to the post and the fiddler his bow, forming an arch. The team forms a chain holding their sticks horizontally and walk round the pole and under the arch formed by the emblem and mute. Then the dancers lie on the ground and the captain, bearing the pole, and followed by the standard bearer, musicians, and lastly the mute, steps over them. I am tempted to wonder if the origin of the Cotswold leapfrog dance was something similar. Then follows the bastinado where each member of the team is struck on the thighs and soles of the feet, the mute striking each man with his emblem. He escapes his beating by a back somersault, but is finally caught and receives his beating to conclude the initiation ceremony.

The next film from Falfani shows the mute disguised as a bull with horns, leading the procession in two instances with a great extended phallus. This is followed by the dancers dancing over the sick children.

From Bukovina comes a New Year's Dance of village boys wearing masks. The characters include an old man carrying the broken wheel of the sun, a Hobby horse and Jew, a Bear Gypsy, a Bride and Groom, and old men who act a mime of harvesting. The Bear and Gypsy dance together, the Hobby horse dances with the Jew, and the Bride with the Groom: the old men work with harvesting forks. The Bear dies, and the Gypsy strikes him gently with two sticks in an effort to bring him to life. He turns him round and tries to pull him up, but the bear falls again. The bear takes the broken wheel of the sun, and is finally turned in reverse to the sun and is revived.

Finally from Slobozia comes another film showing the mute with animal mask and carrying a wooden phallus and crook covered with red binding. The main company dance round their standard, the mute turning somersaults and dancing in his own way. He has taken a pot full of water from a house, and pours the water over his head, throwing the pot high in the air. This was supposed to kill drought. The dancers next form a pyramid, three men high, holding the post, to represent a good harvest with high stacks of corn. This is repeated twice over. The men dance on all fours, face down, and the mute fetches a puppy which he castrates whilst the dance continues. This is not shown on the film. Finally the poles are thrown on to the ground and the men dance with hands on each others' shoulders. The mute drags women from the audience into the field.

The lengthiest action of all these filmed versions is also incomplete because there is no revival. Whether there ever had been in this particular village is not known, but on the evidence from elsewhere it seems a reasonable assumption that there once had been. The behaviour of the performers is such that one cannot question the reluctance of British authorities to permit their continuance had our ceremonials followed the same pattern. Although the Rumanian ceremony as we have seen it was filmed between the two world wars, it was performed by people who were, even at that time, still living in primitive conditions, which accounts for much that is unpalatable to a sophisticated audience. It is extremely unlikely that the Rumanians today would perform the action in the way that we have seen it: indeed, I understand that a casualty of the growth of political awareness has been the Russian, who, as an unpleasant character as we have seen, was unacceptable to the Communist regime.

Apart from its other features of interest I am inclined to regard the enclosure of a space by a ring of linked performers as worthy of special mention. I referred to this particular performance when discussing the sword dance ceremonies, and suggested that the true origin of the linked dances of the north-east of England, might be found in some such action as the Rumanians performed. The space enclosed by there characters is clearly intended to represent a marriage house, the creation of 'doors' and 'windows' as the action demanded is sufficient proof of that if proof were needed. The links held by our north-eastern performers are more likely to have had their origin in something similar than in the carrying of swords which their social position prevented them from ever possessing. The use of such a marriage bower dates from the earliest periods of history: for example, in the early kingdoms of Mesopotamia, a sacred marriage, with parts often played by the king and his daughter, took place inside a fragile 'marriage house' or 'bower.' The sacred marriage was also one of the rituals in the annual cycle of Dionysos, presumably the Roumanian example, and possibly our own sword dance ceremony, have their roots in this same primitive custom.

H

EXTRACT OF A LETTER FROM E. M. LEATHER

The horse's head in Cheshire is still one of the most important features of the Cheshire Souling Play. Its significance as a major "luck-bringing" element is unquestionable. It is not uncommon to come across incidents of one troupe stealing another town's head. A letter contained in the Helm Collection gives us some valuable information on the common kind of piracy that occurs in Cheshire and the making of the head.

The horse's head never belonged to Lymm. It belonged to Warburton and was always kept at the Saracen's Head and Garnett Bauff hired the costumes for the young men of Warburton. The first horse's head was stolen, so two of the men went to Toole's of Warrington and got another head and they boiled it in a boiler at the 'Saracen's Head' and got all the flesh off it. They had to put it together again and glued the teeth in, painted it and decorated it and put it on a wooden leg and put a handle at the back to open its mouth and the man underneath the cloth worked it.[A]

[A] From E. M. Leather to Mrs. Yarwood, November 8, 1950. H.C., III, 396.

I

AN ACCOUNT OF THE MUMMERS, 1793

Among the earliest incidents of life, I recollect seeing, in a remote part of England, one of those sets of irregulars, in that country, called mummers; from which appellation, that outre mode of playing commonly practiced by itinerant actors and sometimes even upon the established theatres, we presume, stiled mumming: It was composed of young men, farmers' sons, and those of decent tradesmen, They had with them, as is customary, a Clown, the ancient fool of the Hall: He had on a patched jacket and trowsers, with a fox's tail to his cap.

The first piece or play, comprised a kind of Harlequin plot, with a father, daughter and two lovers. The fool of the hall carried the lady, to the joy of the rustic audience; the father was reconciled and the lovers made happy.

The interlude represented the staggering of a drunkard, with his glass and bottle; and the conclusion or farce, was compound of some tricks of the fool, who was supposed to be killed, and after being tumbled about in different positions, frightened his companions from the stage, which closed the scene. The amusements of the evening were prefaced with a song, of perhaps thirty stanzas, by way of prologue; the hereditary office, I was given to understand, of the motley fool. The purport of the composition was to announce the performers, who came on one after another, following the Clown in a circle, till the whole, with their characters and abilities, were pointed out to the audience.

From John Jackson, *The History of the Scottish Stage* (Edinburgh, 1793), pp. 410–411.

168

NOTES

NOTES TO PREFACE

1. Antonin Artaud, *The Theater and Its Double* (New York, 1958), p. 37.
2. Richmond Y. Hathorn, *Tragedy, Myth, and Mystery* (Indiana, 1962), p. 19.

NOTES TO CHAPTER I: INVESTIGATING THE ACTION

1. E. K. Chambers, *The English Folk Play* (Oxford, 1933), pp. 4–5.
2. Glynn Wickham, *Early English Stages* (London, 1963), p. 189, is careful to point out the distinction between the folk play and courtly mummings.
3. F. H. Ditchfield, *Old English Customs* (London, 1901), p. 9.
4. E. C. Cawte *et al., English Ritual Drama* (London, 1967).
5. Chambers, pp. 89, 123.
6. Violet Alford, *Introduction to English Folklore* (London, 1952), p. 18.
7. George Ormerod, *History of the County Palatine of Chester,* I (London 1818), lxxix.
8. William Hone, *The Every Day Book,* II (London, 1826), col. 1645–1648.
9. Robert Chambers, *Book of Days,* II (London, 1869), 740–741.
10. Margaret Dean-Smith, "The Life Cycle or Folk Play," *FL,* LXIX (1958), 231.
11. E. K. Chambers, pp. 237–244.
12. The original Ordish papers are housed in the Folk Lore Society Library at the University of London.
13. Arthur W. Beatty, "The St. George Play," *TWAS,* XV (October 1906), 273–324.

14. T. F. Ordish, "Folk Drama," *FL,* II (1891), 214–335; "English Folk Drama," *FL,* IV (1893), 149–175.

15. E. H. Binney, "Oxfordshire Mummers," a transcript of a lecture in front of the Oxford Antiquarian Society, 1902. H.C., VIII, 54–65.

16. Alex Helm, "In Comes I, St. George," *FL,* LXXVI (1965), 118–136.

17. Dean-Smith, pp. 235–236.

18. In a discussion of the play at the Folk Lore Studies Summer Course, Keele University, 1966.

19. *Op. cit.* See especially his discussions of Revesby and Ampleforth, pp. 121–123, 149–150.

20. Thos. Croker, MS. 1206 in Library of Trinity College (Dublin, c. 1800), ch. IX, pp. 11–12.

21. J. Q. Adams, *Chief Pre-Shakespearian Dramas* (Cambridge, 1924), pp. 245–246. See n. 1 for the dating of the references to the play.

22. Extracted by Janet Campbell, November 21, 1957, from the MSS of the Earl of Ancaster at Grimsthorpe in the Lincolnshire Archive Office, Exchequer Gate, Lincoln. H.C., XXIII, 40.

23. A. J. B. Wace, "North Greek Festivals," *BSA,* XVI (1909–1910), 232–253.

24. R. M. Dawkins, "The Modern Carnival in Thrace," JHS, XXVI (1906), 191–206.

25. Violet Alford and Rodney Gallop, *The Traditional Dance* (London, 1935), *passim.*

NOTES TO CHAPTER II: PERFORMING THE ACTION

1. Catherine Cathcart-Smith, "The Soul-Cakers' Play, *JEFDSS,* V (December 1947), 85. H.C., I, 20.

2. In a letter from J. R. Collins of Antrobus (n.d.), H.C., I, 8.

3. Richard Southern, *The Seven Ages of the Theatre* (New York, 1961), p. 55.

4. Margaret Dean-Smith, "Folk Play Origins," *FL,* LXV (1954), 81.

5. See also Enid Welsford, *The Court Masque* (Cambridge, 1927), *passim.*

6. Letter from Catherine Cathcart-Smith, October, 1949. H.C., I, 49.

7. Marie Campbell, "Survival of the Old Folk Drama," *JAF,* LI (January 1938), 11. H.C., XVI, 204.

8. *Ibid.*

9. Southern, pp. 90–98.

10. Arthur Beatty, "The St. George Play," *TWAS,* XV (October 1906), 273–324.

11. Violet Alford, *Sword Dance and Drama* (London, 1966), pp. 203–204.

12. R. R. Marett, "Survival and Revival," *JEFDSS,* I (December 1933), 75.

13. The names of the characters are taken from C. Kille, *The Old Minehead Christmas Mummers Play* (Minehead, 1908), *passim.* H.C., III, 21–48.

14. Southern, p. 38.

15. Helm, *Five Mumming Plays,* p. 3.

16. Tiddy, p. 75.

17. Campbell, p. 11.

18. Peter Kennedy, "The Symondsbury Mumming Play," *JEFDSS,* VII (December 1953), 68. The costume is also shown in Kennedy's film, *Walk in, St. George,* available through the English Folk Dance and Song Society.

19. H.C., II, 370.

20. Helm, *Five Mumming Plays,* plate iv.

21. Theodor Gaster, *Thespis* (New York, 1961), *passim.*

22. See particularly Gilbert Murray, "Excursus on the Origins of Greek Drama," in Jane Ellen Harrison, *Themis* (Cambridge, 1912), pp. 341–363; see also F. M. Cornford, *The Origins of Attic Comedy* (Cambridge, 1914), *passim.*

23. H.C., I, 198.

24. *Ibid.*

25. Archer, p. 35.

26. Netley Abbey, Hampshire. S. Peppler, Esq., MS., January 9, 1893, in Ordish Collection. H.C., V, 120.

27. H.C., II, 352.

28. Collected by Roy Dommett, December 12, 1964. H.C., XXI, 184.

29. *Ibid.,* p. 185.

30. *Ibid.,* p. 186.

NOTES TO CHAPTER III: THE HERO-COMBAT

1. E. H. Binney, MS., September 27, 1907 in Ordish Collection. The bibliographical note reads, "This copy, the Mummers Play, taken from an old MS., date 1780. The MS. was the property of the late Thomas Johnson of Islip, Oxon., and in his handwriting. He was clerk of the parish." H.C., VI, 63.

2. *The Song of Roland,* tr. Dorothy Sayers (Baltimore, 1957), pp. 35–36.

3. Glynn Wickham, *Early English Stages,* I (London, 1963), 18.

4. *Ibid.*

5. *Ibid.,* p. 38.

6. Tiddy, p. 181.

7. Gilbert Murray, "Excursus on Ritual Forms," in Jane Ellen Harrison, *Themis* (Cambridge, 1912), pp. 341–363.

8. E. H. Binney, "The *Alcestis* as Folk Drama," *CR,* XIX (March 1905), 98.

9. Euripides, *The Alcestis,* tr. Gilbert Murray (London, 1936), lines 109–131.

10. Tiddy, p. 213, n.2.

11. Felix Grendon, "The Anglo-Saxon Charms," *JAF,* XXII (April 1909), 111.

12. *Ibid.,* 112–114; see also Lewis Spence, *The Magic Arts in Celtic Britain* (London, 1945), pp. 58–73.

13. Barrow-upon-Humber, Lincolnshire. John Martin, MS., 1951 in Vaughan Williams Library Collection. H.C., IV, 140.

14. Camborne, Cornwall. Tiddy, p. 146.

15. J. Reid, butler, St. Margaret's Bay Hotel, MS. in Ordish Collection (n.d.). H.C., V, 130.

16. Tiddy, p. 76.

17. Overton, Hampshire. Tiddy, p. 197.

18. Peter Kennedy, "The Symondsbury Mumming Play," p. 11.

19. Maud Karpeles, "Some Fragments of the Sword Dance Plays," *JEFDS,* 2nd s., II (1928) 35–42. H.C., I, 272.

20. *The York Cycle of Mystery Plays,* ed. J. S. Purvis (London, 1957), pp. 301–311.

21. Lockinge, Berkshire: Stuart Piggott, "Mummers Plays," 278; Hatford, Berkshire; Alfred Williams Collection in the Swindon Public Library, 1916; Bow, Devonshire: Theo Brown, "The Mummers Play in Devon," *FL,* LXIII (March 1952), 32; High Furness, Lancashire: H.C., XXIII, 4.

22. Douglas Kennedy, "Dramatic Elements in the Folk Dance," *JEFDSS,* VI (1949), 5.

23. Anne Elizabeth Baker, *Glossary of Northamptonshire Words and Phrases,* II (London, 1854), 430. H.C., II, 176–179.

24. Verrier Elwin, "The Hobby Horse and his Ecstatic Dance," *FL,* LIII (1942), 209–213.

25. Peter Kennedy, "The Symondsbury Mumming Play," p. 10.

26. Tiddy, p. 236.

27. George Long, *The Folklore Calendar* (London, 1930), p. 222. H.C., II, 110.

28. H.C., XXII, 33.

29. *Ibid.*

30. *Ibid.*

31. Cornford, pp. 64–66.

32. Helm, *Five Mumming Plays,* p. 30.

33. *Ibid.,* p. 36.

34. Cornford, p. 106.
35. *Ibid.,* p. 105.
36. Helm, *Five Mumming Plays,* pp. 27–28.
37. Cornford, p. 19.
38. Tiddy, p. 70.

NOTES TO CHAPTER IV: THE SWORD PLAY

1. Norman Peacock, "The Greatham Sword Dance," *JEFDSS,* VIII (December 1957), 30–36.
2. *Ibid.,* p. 30.
3. *Ibid.,* p. 31.
4. *Ibid.*
5. *Ibid.,* p. 32.
6. *Ibid.*
7. *Ibid.,* p. 32.
8. *Ibid.,* p. 33.
9. *Ibid.,* p. 34.
10. *Ibid.*
11. *Ibid.,* p. 36.
12. *Ibid.*
13. *Ibid.*
14. Cecil J. Sharp, *Sword Dances,* I (London, 1912), 82–89. H.C., II, 198–204.
15. *Ibid.,* p. 86.
16. Jane Ellen Harrison, *Themis* (Cambridge, 1912), pp. 140–157.
17. *Ibid.,* p. 143.
18. Sharp, p. 86.
19. *Ibid.,* p. 82.
20. H.C., Index, Durham.
21. *Ancient Poems, Ballads and Songs,* ed. Robert Bell (London, 1857), p. 178.
22. Cuthbert Sharpe, *A Bishopricke Garland* (London, 1834), p. 60.
23. Robert Topliffe, *Popular Melodies of the Tyne* (London, 1815), p. 18.
24. Chambers, p. 132.
25. *Ibid.,* p. 136.
26. H.C., Index, Ampleforth, Yorkshire, sheet 2.
27. *William Congreve,* ed. Alex Charles Ewald (London, 1903), pp. 247–251.
28. Chambers, p. 132.
29. Chambers, pp. 135–136.

30. *Ibid.*

31. *Ibid.,* p. 137.

32. *Ibid.,* p. 140.

33. *Ibid.,* p. 141.

34. *Ibid.,* p. 143.

35. *Ibid.*

36. *Ibid.,* p. 144.

37. *Ibid.,* pp. 144–145.

38. *Ibid.,* p. 146.

39. *Ibid.,* p. 148.

40. *Ibid.,* p. 148.

41. Olaus Magnus, *Historia de gentibus septentrionalibus* (1555), Book XV, ch. 23–24. Reproduced in Chambers, *Medieval Stage,* II (Oxford, 1903), 270.

42. Douglas Kennedy, "Some Observations," p. 38.

43. Helm lectures, pp. 103–104.

NOTES TO CHAPTER V: THE WOOING CEREMONY

1. Charles Read Baskerville, "Mummers' Wooing Plays," *MP,* XXI (February 1924), 250–252; Douglas Kennedy, "Dramatic Elements in the Folk Dance," *JEFDSS,* VI (December 1949), 2–4; Margaret Dean-Smith, "The Life Cycle or Folk Play," *FL,* LXIX (1958), 233–236; Alex Helm, "In Comes I, St. George," *FL,* LXXVI (1965), 121.

2. Baskerville, p. 241.

3. *Ibid.,* p. 242.

4. *Ibid.,* p. 250.

5. *Ibid.,* p. 249.

6. Dawkins, *passim.*

7. Sir James Frazer, *The New Golden Bough,* rev. and ed. Theodor Gaster (New York, 1959), pp. 471–587.

8. *Ibid.,* p. 481.

9. *Ibid.*

10. F. M. Cornford, *The Origin of Attic Comedy* (New York, 1961), p. 65.

11. *Ibid.,* pp. 65–66.

12. *Ibid.,* p. 33.

13. Frazer, pp. 536–540.

14. C. R. Baskerville, *The Elizabethan Jig* (Chicago, 1929), p. 250. See also, "Dramatic Aspects," *passim,* and Sir Offley Wakeman, "Rustic Stage Plays in Shropshire," *TSAS,* Series 1, VII (1884), 383–388.

15. Baskerville, "Mummers' Wooing Plays," pp. 266–267, n. 1, reproduces both texts.

16. *Ibid.*, pp. 250–258.

17. *A Pleasante Comedie, called Wily Beguiled,* First Edition at London, printed by H. L. for Clement Knight, 1606, reproduced in.*Three Centuries of Drama: English 1500–1641* (New York, 1956).

18. *Ibid.*

19. Baskerville, "Mummers' Wooing Plays," p. 261.

NOTES TO CHAPTER VI: TRACES OF ANCIENT MYSTERY

1. Norman N. Holland, "Macbeth as Hibernal Giant," *Literature and Psychology,* X (1960), 37–38.

2. Theodor H. Gaster, *Thespis* (New York, 1961), p. 17.

3. *Ibid.*

4. See also, Sir James Frazer, *The New Golden Bough,* rev. and ed. Theodor Gaster (New York, 1959), pp. 35–62, 94–104.

5. Gaster, *Thespis,* p. 17.

6. Harrison, *Themis,* p. 197.

7. *Ibid.*

8. *Ibid.*

9. This is the version discovered by Wilhelm Arndt in 1874, Bollandist Library, Brussels, Codex Gallicanus. It is quoted by John E. Matzke, "Contributions to the History of the Legend of St. George," *PMLA,* XVII (1902), 464.

NOTES TO APPENDIX D

1. T. F. Ordish, "Morrice Dancers at Revesby," *Folk-Lore,* VII (1889), 338.

2. E. K. Chambers, *The English Folk Play* (Oxford, 1933), p. 123.

3. Chambers, *The Medieval Stage,* I (Oxford, 1903), 207.

4. Violet Alford, *Sword Dance and Drama* (London, 1962), p. 54.

5. Chambers, *English Folk Play,* p. 123.

6. John Brand, *Popular Antiquities* (London, 1813), p. 573.

7. Chambers, *English Folk Play,* p. 121.

NOTES TO APPENDIX E

1. Chambers, *The Medieval Stage,* II (Oxford, 1903), p. 276.

2. *Ibid.*, p. 271.

3. *Ibid.*, pp. 271–272.

4. *Ibid.,* p. 276.

5. Norman Peacock, "The Greatham Sword Dance," *JEFDSS,* VIII (December 1956), 31.

6. Chambers, p. 274.

7. *Ibid.,* p. 275.

8. *Ibid.,* p. 273.

9. *Ibid.,* p. 275.

BIBLIOGRAPHY OF WORKS CONSULTED

Addis, John. "St. George and the Dragon," *NQ,* 5th s., I (April 4, 1874), 227.

Addy, S. O. "Guising and Mumming in Derbyshire," *JDA,* XXIX (January 1907), 31–42.

Alford, Violet. *Introduction to English Folklore.* London, 1952.

———. "Review of *Seasonal Feasts and Festivals* by E. O. James," *JEFDSS,* IX (December 1961), 107–108.

———. "Some Hobby Horses of Great Britain," *JEFDSS,* III (December 1939), 221–240.

———. *Sword Dance and Drama.* London, 1962.

Alford, Violet, and Rodney Gallop. "Correspondence to the Editor," *JEFDSS,* III (December 1937), 150–151.

———. *The Traditional Dance.* London, 1935.

[A]mery, P. S. F. "The Christmas Play of St. George," *Western Antiquary,* III (December 1883), 168–169.

Andre, J. Lewis. "St. George the Martyr, in Legend, Ceremonial, Art," *The Archaeological Journal,* LVII (1900), 204–223.

Aram, C. H. "Ipsey, Pipsy, Palsy, Gout," *The Nottinghamshire Countryside,* XVII (Winter 1956–1957), 25–26.

Archer, William. *Real Conversations.* London, 1904.

Arnott, S. "The Christmas Play of *The Seven Champions,*" *NQ,* 5th s., X (December 21, 1878), 489.

Artaud, Antonin. *The Theater and Its Double,* trans. Mary Caroline Richards. New York, 1958.

Aruch, Aldo. "Per l'origine di 'bruscello,'" *Societa di E Inografia Italiana,* IV (1915), 69–74.

Askew, H. "Three Folk Plays," *TYDS,* IV, pt. XXVII (April 1926).

Baker, Anne Elizabeth. *Glossary of Northamptonshire Words and Phrases.* 2 Vols. London, 1854.

Balch, E. E. "In a Wiltshire Village: Some Old Songs and Customs," *The Antiquary,* XLIV (1908), 379–382.

Barley, M. W. "Plough Plays in the East Midlands," *JEFDSS,* VII (December 1953), 68–95.

Barnaschone, L. P. "Manners and Customs of the People of Tenby in the Eighteenth Century," *The Cambrian Journal,* IV (1857), 193–195.

Baskerville, Charles Read, "Dramatic Aspects of Medieval Folk Festivals in England," SP, XVII (1920), 19–87.

———. *The Elizabethan Jig and Related Song Drama.* Chicago, 1929.

———. *English Elements in Jonson's Early Comedy.* Texas, 1911.

———. "Mummers' Wooing Plays in England," *MP,* XXI (February 1924), 225–272.

Beatty, Arthur. "The St. George or Mummers' Play: A Study in the Protology of the Drama," *TWAS,* XV, Pt. 2 (October 1906), 273–324.

Bede, Cuthbert. "Modern Mumming," *NQ,* 2nd s., XI (April 6, 1861), 271.

Bell, Robert, ed. *Ancient Poems, Ballads and Songs of the Peasantry of England.* London, 1857.

Binney, E. H. "The Alcestis as Folk Drama," *The Classical Review,* XIX (March 1905), 18–47.

Boase, George C. "The Padstow May Songs," *Western Antiquary,* VII (June 1887), 46–47.

Boger, J. T. C. "The Play Acted by the Tipteers at West Wittering, Chichester," *SAC,* XLIV (1901), 14–18.

Bowness, E. A. "The Pasche Egging Song," *The Cambria* (N.S.), II (April 1952), 10–11.

Boyd, Arnold W. "The Comberbach (Cheshire) Version of the Soul-Caking Play," *TLCA,* XLIV (1927), 50–55.

———. "The Tichborne Mummers' Play," *CNQ,* CLX (1931), 93–97.

Brand, John. *Observations on Popular Antiquities.* Rev. and ed. Henry Ellis, 2 vols. London, 1841.

Breck, Samuel. *Recollections of Samuel Breck, with Passages from his Notebooks (1771–1862),* ed. H. E. Scudder. Philadelphia, 1877.

Brown, Theo. "The Mummers Play in Devon and Newfoundland," *FL,* LXIII (March 1952), 30–34.

Buchanan, Walter. " 'The Christmas Boys' or 'Mummers,' " *WA,* XXVII (June 1894), 311–314.

Burne, Charlotte S. " 'Guiser's' Play, Songs and Rhymes from Staffordshire," *FLJ,* IV, pt. 4 (1886), 350–357.

Campbell, Marie. "Survivals of Old Folk Drama in the Kentucky Mountains,"
  JAF, LI (January 1938), 10–24.
Carrington, F. A. "On Certain Ancient Wiltshire Customs," *WA*, I (1854),
  79–85.
Cathcart-Smith, Catherine. "Two Variations of the Folk Play and a Further
  Account of the 'Old Hoss'," *JEFDSS*, V (December 1947), 81–91.
Cawte, E. C., Alex Helm, and Norman Peacock. *English Ritual Drama.* Lon-
  don, 1967.
Cawte, E. C., Alex Helm, R. J. Marriott, and Norman Peacock. "A Geographi-
  cal Index of the Ceremonial Dance in Great Britain," *JEFDSS*, IX
  (December 1960), 1–41.
Chalk, Edwin S. "The Silverton Mummers' Play," *DNQ*, IX (1916–1917),
  228–232.
Chambers, E. K. *The English Folk Play.* Oxford, 1933.
————. *The Medieval Stage.* 2 Vols. Oxford, 1903.
Chambers, Robert. *Book of Days.* 2 Vols. London, 1869.
————. *Popular Rhymes of Scotland.* Edinburgh, 1841.
Chaucer, Geoffrey. *The Poetical Works of Chaucer,* ed. F. N. Robinson.
  Cambridge, Mass., 1933.
Cherry, Mary G. "The Plough Monday Play in Rutland," *RMC*, I (January
  1903–October 1904), 195–199.
Cocks, Alfred Heneage. "The Wooburn Version of the Mummers' Play,"
  Records of Buckinghamshire, IX (1909), 222–226.
Cook, T. D. "A Northumbrian Sword Dance," *JEFDSS*, I (December 1933),
  111–112.
Cornford, Francis Macdonald. *The Origin of Attic Comedy,* ed. Theodor H.
  Gaster. Garden City, N.Y., 1961.
Crowther-Beynon, V. B. "Morris Dancers Play-Edith Weston, Rutland," *RMC*,
  II (1905–1906), 177–180.
Dawkins, R. M. "The Modern Carnival in Thrace and the Cult of Dionysus,"
  JHS, XXVI (1906), 191–218.
Dean-Smith, Margaret. "Folk Play Origins of the English Masque," *FL*, LXV
  (1954), 74–86.
————. "A Note on Richard Johnson's *Famous History of the Seven
  Champions*," *JEFDSS*, VII (December 1954), 180–181.
————. "The Life Cycle or Folk Play," *FL*, LXIX (1958), 237–253.
————. *An Unromantic View of the Mummers' Play.* London, 1966.
Denham, Michael Aislabie. *The Denham Tracts,* ed. James Hardy. 2 Vols.
  London, 1895.
Ditchfield, F. H. *Old English Customs.* London, 1901.

Douce, Francis. *Illustrations of Shakespeare and of Ancient Manners.* London, 1839.

Douglas, George William. *American Book of Days,* rev. Helen Douglas Compton. New York, 1948.

Dowson, Frank W. "Notes on the Goathland Folk Play," *TYDS,* XXVIII (April 1926), 36–37.

———. "Wood-lore, Practices and Beliefs in Blackamore," *TYDS,* XXXVIII (1938), 33–35.

Durkheim, Émile. *The Elementary Forms of the Religious Life,* trans. Joseph Ward Swain. New York, 1915.

Ebsworth, J. W. "A Garland of Christmas Carols with an Overture of Christmas Mummers," *NQ,* 5th s., X (December 21, 1878), 484–489.

Elwin, Verrier. "The Hobby Horse and the Ecstatic Dance," *FL,* LIII (1942), 209–213.

Evans-Pritchard, E. E. *Essays in Social Anthropology.* New York, 1963.

Fallow, T. M. "Yorkshire Sword Actors," *The Antiquary,* XXXI (May 1895), 138–142.

Farnell, Lewis Richard. *The Cults of the Greek States.* 5 Vols. Oxford, 1909.

Frazer, Sir James George. *The Golden Bough; a Study in Magic and Religion.* 12 Vols. London, 1911–1915.

———. *The New Golden Bough,* ed. and rev. Theodor H. Gaster. New York, 1959.

Freud, Sigmund. *Totem and Taboo,* trans. James Strachery. London, 1950.

Gailey, Alan. "The Folk Play in Ireland," *Studia Hibernica,* VI (1966), 113–154.

———. *Irish Folk Drama.* Cork, 1968.

———. "The Rhymers of South-East Antrim," *Ulster Folklife,* XIII (1967), 18–28.

———. "Straw Costume in Irish Folk Customs," *Folk Life,* VI (1968), 83–93.

Gallop, Rodney. "The Origins of the Morris Dance," *JEFDSS,* I (December 1934), 122–129.

Gaster, Theodor H. *Thespis.* Garden City, 1961.

Gatty, Ivor. "The Eden Collection of Mumming Plays," *FL,* LIX (1948), 225–290.

Gomme, Alice Bertha. *The Traditional Games of England, Scotland, and Ireland.* 2 Vols. London, 1894.

Grendon, Felix. "The Anglo-Saxon Charms," *JAF,* XXII (April–June 1909), 105–237.

Halliwell, James Orchard. *Contributions to Early English Literature.* London, 1849.

Hannam-Clark, Theodore. *Drama in Gloucestershire (The Cotswold Country).* London, 1928.

Harman, H. *Sketches of the Buckinghamshire Countryside.* London, 1934.

Harrison, Jane Ellen. *Prolegomena to the Study of Greek Religion.* Cambridge, 1908.

———. *Themis, A Study of the Social Origins of Greek Religion.* Cambridge, 1912.

Hartland, E. Sidney. *The Legend of Perseus.* 3 Vols. London, 1896.

Hathorn, Richmond Y. *Tragedy, Myth, and Mystery.* Indiana, 1966.

Haworth, D., and W. M. Comber, eds., *Cheshire Village Memories.* Cheshire, 1952.

Helm, Alex. "The Cheshire Soul Caking Play," *JEFDSS,* VII (December 1950), 45–50.

———. Collection. 35 Vols. Congleton, Cheshire.

———. *Five Mumming Plays for Schools.* London, 1965.

———. "In Comes I, St. George," *FL,* LXXVI (1965), 118–136.

———. Lectures at Keele University, MS., 1966.

———, and E. C. Cawte. *Six Mummers' Acts.* Leicestershire, 1967.

Henderson, William. *Notes on the Folk Lore of the Northern Counties of England and the Borders.* London, 1866.

H[ole], C[hristina]. "The North Newington Mumming Play," *ODF,* VIII (1956) 14–15.

Holland, Norman N. "Macbeth as Hibernal Giant," *Literature and Psychology,* X (1960), 37–38.

Holland, Robert. *A Glossary of Words in the County of Chester.* 3 Vols. London, 1884–1886.

Holmes, J. G. "Plough Monday Plays," *The Nottinghamshire Countryside,* XIII (January 1952), 7–8.

Hone, William. *The Every Day Book.* 2 Vols. London, 1826.

Hooke, S. H., ed. *Myth, Ritual and Kingship.* Oxford, 1958.

Hudleston, N. A. "The Ebberston Mummers Play," *JEFDSS,* VII (December 1953), 130–131.

Hyman, Stanley Edgar. *The Tangled Bank.* New York, 1962.

Jackson, Georgina F. *Shropshire Folk-Lore,* ed. Charlotte Sophia Bourne. London, 1883.

Jackson, John. *The History of the Scottish Stage.* Edinburgh, 1793.

James, E. O. *Sacrifice and Sacrament.* London, 1962.

Jenkinson, A. J. "Ploughboys Play," *The Cornhill Magazine* N.S., LXVIII (1930), 96–105.

John, Gwen. "The Derbyshire Mumming Play of St. George and The Dragon;

or, as it is sometimes called, The Pace Egg," *FL*, XXXII (1921), 181–193.

Johnson, Richard. *The Renowned History of the Seven Champions of Christendom*. London, 1824.

Jones, Bryan. "Christmas Mumming in Ireland," *FL*, XXVII (1916), 301–307.

Karpeles, Maud. "Some Fragments of Sword Dance Plays," *JEFDS*, 2nd s., II (1928), 35–42.

Kennedy, Douglas. "Dramatic Elements in the Folk Dance," *JEFDSS*, VI (1949), 1–7.

———. "Observations on the Sword Dance and Mummers Play," *JEFDS* (2nd s.), III (1930), 36–37.

Kennedy, Patrick. *The Banks of the Boro, A Chronicle of the County of Wexford*. London, 1867.

Kennedy, Peter. "The Symondsbury Mumming Play," *JEFDSS*, VII (December 1952), 1–12.

Kettlewell, F. B. *Trinkum-Trinkums of Fifty Years*. Taunton. 1927

Kille, C. *The Old Minehead Christmas Mummers Play*. Minehead, 1908.

Kirke, John. "The Seven Champions of Christendom," ed. G. Dawson. *Western Reserve University Bulletin* (N.S.), XXXII.

Lack-Szyrma, W. S. "Christmas Play of St. George," *Western Antiquary*, III (January 1884), 198.

Leather, Ella Mary. *The Folklore of Herefordshire*. Hereford, 1912.

Lee, Frederick George. "Oxfordshire Christmas Miracle Play," *NQ*, 5th s. II (December 26, 1874), 503–505.

Lévi-Strauss, Claude. *Structural Anthropology*, trans. Claire Jacobson and Brooke Grundfest Schoepf. New York, 1963.

Long, George. *The Folklore Calendar*. London, 1930.

Lowe, Barbara. "Early Records of the Morris in England," *JEFDSS*, VIII (December 1957), 61–82.

Lowie, Robert H. *Primitive Religion*. New York, 1924.

MacNamara, Margaret. "A Christmas Mummers' Play," *Drama*, X (December 1931), 42–44.

MacTaggart, John. *The Scottish Gallovidian Encyclopedia*. London, 1824.

Maidment, James. *Galatians*. Edinburgh, 1835.

Manly, John Matthews. *Specimens of the Pre-Shakespearean Drama*, I. London, 1897.

Marett, R. R. *Psychology and Religion*. London, 1920.

———. "Survival and Revival," *JEFDSS*, I (December 1933), 73–78.

Marshall, John J. *Popular Rhymes and Sayings of Ireland*. Dungannon, 1931.

Matzke, John E. "Contributions to the History of the Legend of St. George, Part I," *PMLA*, XVII, IV (1902), 464–535.

————. "Contributions to the History of the Legend of St. George, Part II," *PMLA*, XVII, 1 (1903), 99–156.

————. "The Legend of Saint George; Its Development into a *Roman d'Aventure*," *PMLA*, XIX, III (1904), 449–478.

McCaughan, Michael. "Christmas Rhymers in the Donaghadee Area," *Ulster Folklife*, XIV (1968), 66–70.

Mead, Margaret and Nicholas Calas, eds. *Primitive Heritage*. New York, 1953.

Meynell, Rosemary. "Come, Brave Bow Slash and His Men," *The Derbyshire Countryside*, XXIII (December 1957), 22–23, 35.

Miles, Clement A. *Christmas in Ritual and Tradition, Christian and Pagan*. London, 1912.

Murray, Gilbert. *Five Stages of Greek Religion*. Oxford, 1925.

Myres, M. W. "The Frodsham Soul-Caking Play," *FL*, XLIII (1932), 97–104.

Needham, Joseph. "The Geographical Distribution of English Ceremonial Dance Traditions," *JEFDSS*, III (December 1936), 1–45.

Needham, Joseph, and Arthur L. Peck. "Molly Dancing in East Anglia," *JEFDSS*, I (December 1933), 79–85.

Neumann, Erich. *The Origins and History of Consciousness*. 2 Vols. New York, 1954.

Newhouse, Clare and Mildred Dennis. "Christmas Mummers' Play from Bisley, Gloucestershire," *FL*, XLVI (1935), 361–365.

Newman, F. "Mummers' Play from Middlesex," *FL*, XLI (1930), 95–98.

Onians, Richard Broxton. *The Origins of European Thought*. Cambridge, 1954.

Ordish, T. F. *Collection*. University of London, Folklore Society Library.

————. "English Folk-Drama," *FL*, IV (1893), 149–175.

————. "Folk Drama," *FL*, II (1891), 314–335.

————. "Morris Dance at Revesby," *FLJ*, VII (1889), 331–356.

Ormerod, George. *History of The County Palatine of Chester*. London, 1818.

Ovid. *Fasti*. Trans. Sir James George Frazer. London, 1903.

Parish, W. D. *A Dictionary of the Sussex Dialect*. London, 1875.

Parker, Angelina. "Oxfordshire Village Folklore, 1840–1900," *FL*, XXIV (1913), 86–87.

Patterson, W. H. "The Christmas Rhymers in the North of Ireland," *NQ*, 4th s., X (December 21, 1872), 487–488.

Peacock, Mabel. "Plough Monday Mummeries," *NQ*, 9th s., VII (April 27, 1901), 322–324.

Peacock, Norman. "The Greatham Sword Dance," *JEFDSS*, VIII (December 1956), 29–39.

Persson, Axel W. *The Religion of Greece in Prehistoric Times.* Berkeley, 1942.

Pickard-Cambridge, A. W. *Dithyramb Tragedy and Comedy.* Oxford, 1927.

Piggott, Stuart. "Mummers' Plays from Berkshire, Derbyshire, Cumberland and the Isle of Man," *FL,* XXXIX (1928), 271–279.

Pollard, Alfred W. *English Miracle Plays, Moralities and Interludes.* Oxford, 1927.

Purvis, J. S. *Tudor Parish Documents in the Diocese of York.* Cambridge, 1948.

Ratcliffe, Thomas. "Mumming Play, Derbyshire," *NQ,* 10th s., VII (January 12, 1907), 31–32.

Ridgeway, William. *The Dramas and Dramatic Rituals of Non-European Races,* Cambridge, 1915.

———. *The Origin of Tragedy.* Cambridge, 1910.

Rouse, W. H. D. "Christmas Mummers at Rugby," *FL,* X (1899), 186–194.

Rudkin, E. H. "Lincolnshire Plough Play," *FL,* L (1939), 88–97.

Sargent, Helen Child and George Lyman Kittredge, eds., *English and Scottish Popular Ballads.* Boston, 1904.

Sawyer, Frederick E. "Sussex Tipteerers' Play," *FLJ,* II (1884), 1–7.

Schechner, Richard. "Approaches to Theory/Criticism," *TDR,* X (Summer 1966), 20–53.

Schmidt, Leopold. *Das Deutsche Volksschauspiel: Ein Handbuch.* Berlin, 1962.

Sharp, Cecil J. *Field Notebooks.* Clare College, Cambridge (Microfilm copies in Vaughan Williams Library, Cecil Sharpe House, London).

———. *Sword Dances of Northern England.* 3 Vols. London, 1912.

Sharp, Cuthbert. *The Bishoprick Garland.* London, 1834.

Smith, Alan. "A West Kent Christmas Mummers' Play," *KCJ,* VII (1947), 97–98.

Smith, G. Gregory. *The Transition Period.* New York, 1900.

Southern, Richard. *The Seven Ages of the Theatre.* New York, 1961.

Spence, Lewis. *The Magic Art in Celtic Britain.* New York, [ca. 1945.]

Stevens, Joseph. *A Parochial History of St. Mary Bourne.* London, 1888.

Strutt, Joseph. *Sports and Pastimes of the People of England.* London, 1876.

Taylor, Antoinette. "An English Christmas Play," *JAF,* XXII (1909), 389–394.

Thurston, Peter. "St. George Mummers Plays," *NQ,* 12th s., I (May 13, 1916) 390–393.

Tiddy, R. J. E. *The Mummers' Play.* Oxford, 1923.

Tod, David. "The Mummers Play," *The Gloucestershire Countryside,* II (July 1935), 62–63.

Toschi, Paolo. *Dal Dramma Liturgico Alla Rappresentazione Sacra.* Firenze, 1940.

Udal, J. S. "Christmas Mummers in Dorsetshire," *NQ,* 5th s., II (December 26, 1874), 505.

Utley, Francis Lee. "Folklore, Myth, and Ritual," in *Critical Approaches To Medieval Literature,* ed. Dorothy Bethurum. New York, 1960.

Wace, A. J. B. "Mumming Plays in the Southern Balkans," *BSA,* XIX (1912–1913), 248–265.

———. "North Greek Festivals and the Worship of Dionysus," *BSA,* XVI (1909–1910), 232–253.

Wakeman, Sir Offley. "Rustic Stage Plays in Shropshire," *TSA,* 1st s., VII (1884), 383–388.

Walker, J. C. "Historical Essay on the Irish Stage," *Transactions of the Royal Irish Academy,* II (1788), 75–90.

———. *Historical Memoirs of the Irish Bard.* Dublin, 1786.

Weisinger, Herbert. *Tragedy and the Paradox of the Fortunate Fall.* London, 1953.

Welsford, Enid. *The Court Masque.* Cambridge, 1927.

———. *The Fool, His Social and Literary History.* Garden City, 1961.

Whiting, C. E. "A Plough Monday Play," *DJ,* XXIV (December 1923), 39–43.

Wickham, Glynne. *Early English Stages.* 2 Vols. London, 1963.

Wilson, Edward Meryon. "An Unpublished Version of the Pace-eggers' Play," *FL,* XLIX (1938), 36–44.

Wolfram, Richard. "Ritual and Dramatic Associations of Sword and 'Chain' Dances," *JEFDSS,* II (1935), 35–41.

———. "Sword Dances and Secret Societies," *JEFDSS,* I (December 1932), 34–41.

INDEX OF CHARACTERS
AND PLAYS IN ENGLAND